The Synoptic Gospels

Bro Keith,
I hope This study in
Enrich your Knowledge in
The word. The Lord bless
you as you Study.
Pastor Jackson

The Synoptic Gospels

CONFLICT and CONSENSUS

Keith F. Nickle

John Knox Press
ATLANTA

Library of Congress Cataloging in Publication Data
Nickle, Keith Fullerton, 1933–
    The Synoptic Gospels.

    Bibliography: p.
    1. Bible. N.T. Gospels—Criticism, interpretation, etc. I. Title.
BS2555.2.N486   226'.06   79–92069
ISBN 0–8042–0422–5 (pbk.)

© copyright John Knox Press 1980
10 9 8 7 6
Printed in the United States of America
John Knox Press
Atlanta, Georgia 30365

To Marie, my best friend

Wenn ich alle Weiber der Welt ansche, so finde ich keine, von der ich rühmen könnte, wie ich von meiner mit fröhlichem Gewissen rühmen kann; diese hat mir Gott selbst geschenkt, und ich weiss, dass Ihm samt allen Engeln wohlgefällt, wenn ich mit Liebe und Treue zu ihr halte.

Martin Luther concerning Katie

Preface

Important advances have been made in the study of the Gospels of the New Testament in recent years. Scholars have learned to address new questions to those documents. They have found more thorough ways to ask old questions. Text criticism, literary criticism, form criticism, redaction criticism, tradition criticism—all are terms they have used to describe questions they have found helpful to ask as they try to understand the nature and purpose of the Gospels.

Much of this conversation occurs between professional biblical scholars. What does filter down to the non-specialist is, frequently, so fragmentary, or cryptic or patronizing that it serves more to confuse and to alienate than to clarify.

My purpose in writing this book is to invite the non-specialist to benefit from some of the results of technical scholarly inquiry. I sketch the process by which the earliest Christians retold selectively some of the stories they remembered about Jesus. We consider how they, and other early Christians after them, interpreted and adapted those stories to meet the needs of their communities.

We inquire after the motives and the concerns which prompted each of the first three Evangelists to compose their narrative versions of the public ministry and death of Jesus.

The book does not try to encompass the content of the Gospels of Matthew, Mark, and Luke. Rather, it places before the reader preliminary considerations which will inform and enrich those reflections that occur as the content of the documents is investigated. So the book is really a prelude, a preface to Gospel study.

Those familiar with recent Gospel research will recognize how indebted I am to a host of New Testament scholars. In a work of this kind the dependency is so great and so widespread that every debt simply cannot be acknowledged. Nevertheless my gratitude is at least as great as my debt.

I would like to thank Dr. Richard Ray of John Knox Press for his midwifery of the project and Ms. Joan Crawford for her technical assistance. I am also grateful to Ms. Elsie Urie for her efficient typing of portions of the text. Finally, my special thanks to my wife who not only helped with the typing but also greatly facilitated the composition, and to whom this book is dedicated.

Contents

CHAPTER ONE
Gospel Beginnings

The first four books in the New Testament section of the Bible are known as "Gospels." Each of these books, in its own way, relates incidents out of the life and ministry of Jesus of Nazareth. He lived during the first third of the first century, C.E. (C.E. is the abbreviation for Common Era, that part of human history which Judaism shares in common with Christianity. It refers to the same period of time as did the older abbreviation A.D.) According to the information in the Gospels he was executed during the administration of Pontius Pilate, who was the Roman procurator in Judea from 26–36, C.E. Although the exact date is not certain, Jesus is assumed to have been crucified around 30 C.E.

Where did the four Gospels come from? Why were they written? Where did their authors obtain the information they included in their Gospel narratives? The four Gospels traditionally have been regarded as written by Matthew, a tax collector and one of the Twelve; Mark, an assistant to Peter; Luke, a companion of Paul; and John, a son of Zebedee and one of the Twelve. Are those traditions dependable, and, if not, who actually wrote each of the four Gospels?

In this chapter we will consider the formation of the Christian church, the gospel message it preached, the cultural contexts within which it moved, the nature and forms of oral tradition, the different uses of the term "gospel," and some general observations about Gospel authorship.

I. THE EARLY CHURCH AND ITS PREACHING

A. *The Formation of the Christian Church*

Our knowledge of the first days of the Christian church is very limited. Information about the earliest stages in the life of the Christian fellowship which formed after the resurrection is meager. Actually that is true not only of the beginnings of the church but also for its first one hundred years of existence.[1] It seems strange that that is so, especially strange when we realize that that is precisely the period within which all of the documents which make up the New Testament were written.

The problem of scanty information about the beginning decades in the church's history is aggravated by the limited sources. All of the information we have comes from documents produced by the church itself. And those documents were written to meet other needs and purposes than to satisfy our curiosity about what really happened way back then.

Important as it is to recognize the limits of the sources available to us we must not become too discouraged. A careful examination of early Christian literature discloses much information to help us recover aspects of the earliest Christian experience.[2] Furthermore, scholars have studied the first century, C.E., intensely. We may use the results of their study to reconstruct major features of the civilization and cultures of the first century world within which the church developed.

It seems certain to most New Testament scholars that Jesus did not organize the church as a religious institution during the period of his public ministry. Rather the relationship he fostered between himself and his intimate followers was modeled in some ways on the relationship which existed in Judaism between the rabbi (Jewish expert on the the Torah, the holy law of Moses) and his followers, his disciples. Yet there were important differences. Jesus did not educate his disciples to become rabbis themselves. Rather he offered them the possibility to share his own destiny—of being agents through whom God's right and intent to rule redemptively in his creation was proclaimed. To that end he formed them together into an intimate fellowship of itinerant preachers and healers.[3]

His followers regarded the crucifixion of Jesus as a tragically ruthless murder. Nonetheless they were convinced that this did not thwart but instead accomplished the saving purposes of God. Quite soon after his execution his followers showed themselves to be persuaded that God had raised him from the dead.

The explanation they offered for this persuasion was the appearances of Jesus to them after his burial.[4] They understood and described these appearances as more than just ecstatic, visionary experiences. They were occasions by which God was revealing Jesus to them as the Risen One, his chosen agent for eternal life, and thereby was revealing himself as the Giver of Life. They had known and worshiped God as the Giver of Life previously. But the raising of Jesus from the dead was the manifestation "par excellence" by God of himself as Life-giver.

As far as we can tell from the New Testament documents all of the first Christians were Jews. That is because Jesus' own ministry was limited to Galilee and Judea, both Jewish areas. The disciples he gathered around him were Jews. Consequently the community they formed after the resurrection, that is the church in its earliest stages, was a sect within Judaism. They continued to observe and participate in Jewish cultic practices. They shared many of the convictions, hopes, beliefs, and prejudices of religious Jews. The major distinctive feature of their religious faith was their belief that Jesus was the Messiah whom God had upheld and vindicated with the resurrection.

The first Christians, the Jewish Christians, found confirmation for their belief in the correspondence of their experience with the expectations of Jewish Scriptures. The Jews believed that the spirit of God had been uniquely with God's people, Israel, from the time of the Patriarchs and of Moses through the time of the prophets. But then the presence of his spirit had been withdrawn. Their Scriptures anticipated that the time of the Messiah would be the time when God would return the presence of his spirit to Israel. The first Christians were convinced that the spirit of prophecy had been restored by God as a feature of their community life.

Related to that conviction was the persuasion of the Jewish Christians that they were living in the last days before God brought this world to an end. Their Jewish heritage had taught them that the appearance of the Messiah and the return of God's spirit to his people were signs of the last days. It was anticipated by the Jews that God would restore his whole creation to the perfection of Eden (the world when first created in perfect harmony with the rule of God).

The first Christians believed that God was active among them creating his end-of-time people. They were to inherit the blessings of the new age when God brought the age of this world to a close. They had been chosen to participate in God's new creation over which he would rule as he had in Eden.

B. The Church's Preaching

The Jewish Christian church lived then much as did any other Jewish sect community. Of course, its lifestyle did reflect the belief that God had poured out his spirit upon Christian believers (the technical term is "charismatic"). But more than that, the earliest Christians believed that God wanted them to tell others that the end of this world was near, that Jesus was the end-time Messiah, that God was reasserting his right to rule. So they devoted much of their energy and efforts to preaching about these distinctively Christian beliefs.

Early Christian preaching developed in two directions. The church sought to continue and extend the message which the disciples had heard Jesus preach during his own ministry: "the kingdom of God is at hand" (Mark 1:15; cf. Matt. 10:7). But the early church also increased the content of the message to include preaching about Jesus himself.

Jewish traditions held that after God had created the world it became alienated from him because of human sin. God desired to overcome that alienation. He chose Israel as the people out of which he would bring a Deliverer and Savior. The early church declared that Jesus was the chosen agent through whom God had worked, was working, and would continue to work to accomplish his intent to save his estranged creation.

Since the people to whom the first Christians preached were also Jews they shared a common religious heritage. "Messiah" was the Jewish term for the expected Deliverer sent by God. (It comes from the Hebrew word meaning "to anoint." Jews believed that God anointed his agents to accomplish special tasks.) By the time of Jesus, Jewish hopes for the coming of the Messiah had been held for a long time. The type of Deliverer that the Messiah would be was disputed. Some Jews looked for a martial figure who would lead the forces of Israel to overthrow the armies of foreign oppression. Others looked for a political leader who would restore the international prestige and economic prosperity of Israel to the splendor of King David's reign. Still others expected the Messiah to be similar to some of its great religious leaders in the past—Moses, or Elijah, or another of the prophets.

When the first Christians preached that Jesus was the Messiah they were using a term which everyone knew. But it was extremely ambiguous as a description of the function and identity of Jesus in God's saving plan. "What do you mean by Messiah?" their Jewish listeners wanted to know. "Is he another King David?" "Is he Moses returned to be with us?" "Is he a prophet of the end of the world?" So they pressed Jewish Christian preachers for an explanation clarifying in what sense they understood Jesus to be Messiah.

C. The Traditions About Jesus

One of the most helpful ways the early church had of responding to questions from the Jews was to tell stories about Jesus. These stories were based for the most part on recollections which his disciples had of events that had happened or things that had been said during their association with Jesus. Those "stories from life" were dramatic, lively, vividly concrete ways of clarifying the meaning of "Messiah" as it applied to Jesus.

The interpretive purposes for which the early church used stories about Jesus affected the selective process. Those stories which spoke most directly to questions that were being asked, those narratives which seemed to call forth the clearest understanding, were the stories used most frequently. Other stories, interesting as they were in their own right, were not retold so often. Certainly some were simply forgotten.

In its preaching the early church was not primarily interested in informing its Jewish listeners about what Jesus had done or who he had been. Rather the Christian missionary preacher was concerned to describe to his listeners what Jesus was doing right then and who Jesus was. That does not mean that the early church was indifferent to its remembrances about what Jesus did and what he said during his lifetime. The first Christians were greatly interested in that. But the stories about Jesus which held the most enduring fascination were those stories which explained the messianic identity of Jesus and pointed to his continuing, present activity. That is what really interested them, that is what they were so eager to communicate to the Jews hearing their preaching. They chose those stories about Jesus which were the most convincing and persuasive.

Missionary motives imposed a selective process on the traditions about Jesus that were preserved. Stories which served ordinary curiosity about Jesus' life and ministry but which did not serve to promote belief in Jesus as Messiah were stressed less. Their preaching was intended to stimulate faith. The appropriate response was not so much intellectual comprehension as decision, resulting in commitment of life.

It is hard for us to understand why the early church was not more concerned to preserve and pass on for the benefit of later generations every bit of information it could collect about Jesus. But the first century world and particularly first century Jews were not that interested in objective biography for its own sake. Further, except for the opinions of Christians themselves, Jesus was not yet all that famous. The first Christians were convinced that the last days of the existence of God's creation in the present order had begun. They were not expecting any later generations. They had no motive to preserve every detail of Jesus' life for future ages.

When the early Christian announced to a missionary audience that Jesus was the Messiah-Christ, the Lord, that Christian had to be prepared to answer questions. "Jesus" was a fairly common name. Which "Jesus" was meant? "Messiah" was a title having several contradictory meanings. What kind of "messiah" was the person talking about? "Lord" was a term which could encompass anything from a polite form of address to implications of divinity. What was the nature and source of the lordly authority of Jesus? Traditions about his birth, his home, his family helped to distinguish which "Jesus" the preacher was talking about. The genealogies, the allusions to scriptural descriptions of Davidic messiah, of the suffering One of God, of the Moses servant-prophet served to explain the content of "Messiah." Stories about Jesus' driving out demons, or performing nature miracles, or stories of his baptism and transfiguration served to illustrate that the source of his lordly authority was God.

As we have seen, Christian preaching which began in two directions soon merged those directions. The early church combined the message which Jesus had preached of the re-establishment of God's kingly rule in his creation with its own preaching of Jesus as the Messiah. In the person and activity of the Messiah, Jesus (or, "the Christ, Jesus"—"Christ" is the Greek equivalent to the Hebrew "Messiah"), God again rules his creation. God has demonstrated the reality of his rule by raising Jesus from the dead after a hostile creation destroyed him.

Jews who heard such Christian preaching were often shocked and appalled. If the Christian claims were true why was it necessary for the Christ to suffer and be condemned to die on a cross? Why had the Jewish religious leaders, the representatives of God's own people, judged the Messiah of God to be guilty of blasphemy? How could it be that God would allow such to occur?

To respond to such protests the Jewish Christians appealed to passages in Jewish Scriptures. The Law and the Prophets foretold the fate of Jesus. Many of the events in his life corresponded to predictions in the Jewish Scriptures which had been interpreted as referring to the Messiah. The incidents which occurred during the last days of Jesus in Jerusalem were especially significant in this regard. Think of all the events in those final days that the church believed were in fulfillment of inspired Scripture. They included Jesus' entry into Jerusalem, the cleansing of the Temple, the amount of money Judas received to betray Jesus, the use to which that money was finally put, Jesus' betrayal, his condemnation, the desertion by his disciples, his arrest, trial, crucifixion, and resurrection.

All these moments in the Passion of Jesus fulfilled prophecies in the Jewish Scriptures. These scriptural predictions were weighty evidence for the questioning Jew that God was revealing Jesus as the Messiah through his death and resurrection. The Jewish Scriptures testified that God had already revealed through his prophets that he intended to accomplish his saving purposes in this manner.

The early church did not limit its telling of the Jesus traditions just to the missionary situation. It made broader use of those stories than simply to respond to questions raised by listeners to its gospel preaching. As the church succeeded in preaching the gospel it found increased occasions for employing and adapting stories about Jesus.

New converts required instruction in the basic beliefs of the Christian faith. The story of the great commandment (Mark 12:28–34) was a tradition that would have been useful for catechetical (instructional) purposes. Other Jesus stories assisted the church as it produced patterns of worship. Traditions such as the Lord's Prayer (Matt. 6:9–15) or the Last Supper (Mark 14:17–25) aided in the development of liturgical forms for worship. When Christians became discouraged at the slow and erratic response their preaching produced from non-Christians, the account of Jesus' telling of the Parable of the Soils (Mark 4:1–20) gave comfort and encouragement. Solutions to critical ethical crises arising in the life of the Christian community were stimulated by such stories as Jesus' instructions about divorce (Luke 16:18), or his teachings on humility (Luke 14:7–14), or his advice on church discipline (Matt. 18:15–20). Other traditions inspired and supported Christians who held firm to their beliefs in times of suffering from persecution (cf. Luke 6:27–36; Mark 8:34—9:1; 13:9–13). Stories about Jesus helped the church address concrete issues and problems of the time.

Given the reasons why the early church remembered and passed on its recollections of the earthly ministry of Jesus and given the purposes for which they were employed, it is clear that it is impossible to speak of *the author* of these traditions, or even of any particular tradition. In the modern understanding of authorship they are anonymous. In most instances there is little reason to doubt that they originated with the first disciples who had been intimately associated with Jesus during his lifetime. But there is no way for us to ascribe a particular tradition to a specific disciple with certainty. They were told and retold by too many Christians on too many occasions over too extended a period of time. The whole Christian community is the author of the Jesus tradition. "Its creator is the community; its custodian is the community; and its guarantor is the community."[5]

II. CULTURAL CONTEXTS FOR PREACHING AND TEACHING

Up until now we have been considering the church's use of stories about Jesus as if the only period involved was the first eight or ten years in the life of the church. It's as though the traditions about Jesus were preserved in their pre-literary form by a Jewish Christian church trying to persuade other Jews to believe as they did. But it is more complicated than that.

The interval of time between the church's beginnings and the composition of the Gospels in the New Testament was longer. Scholars estimate the time span to have been thirty-five years or more. During that time major changes took place in the membership of the growing Christian church. Although they were mostly Jews in the beginning, thirty-five years later Christians were mostly Gentile (non-Jews). The language in which preaching and teaching was done changed from Aramaic (the everyday language of Judea) to Greek. The cultural backgrounds of those to whom Christians preached shifted from Semitic (of the Near-Eastern area) to Hellenistic (the Greco-Roman culture of the Mediterranean world).

A. Stages in the Development of Tradition

The initial stage of Christianity might be called Palestinian, Aramaic-speaking Christianity. It was centered on Jerusalem and the Christian community which had formed there. Those belonging to the church were Jews who believed that Jesus was the Messiah sent by God. The disciples who had been associated with Jesus during his life formed the core of the fellowship. Through their preaching and teaching other Jews were persuaded to accept the same belief and join their community.

Although most of the first Christians spoke Aramaic there may have been a few Hellenistic Jews who also believed. (We will discuss who these Hellenistic Jews were in the next paragraphs.) The people to whom they preached were mostly Aramaic-speaking Jews. They could therefore assume acquaintance with Jewish religious traditions and acceptance of Jewish beliefs. Since they preached and taught in Aramaic, the stories about Jesus which they told were told in Aramaic.

Christianity did not remain confined to Aramaic-speaking Palestine for long. It moved out of the bounds of the geographical area around Jerusalem and spread through the region of Judea to Samaria, Damascus, Antioch, and beyond. A number of factors caused this spread. Christians traveled from Jerusalem for business or other purposes. Persecution of Jewish Christians in Jerusalem by hostile non-Christian Jews drove some Christians out. The strong sense of urgency to preach to as many as possible in view of the impending end of the world stimulated others to carry the gospel message to new regions.

The hearers of Christian preaching were still Jews. But they were Hellenistic Jews. Hellenistic Jews were Jews whose family had moved from Palestine into a Greek-speaking area of the Roman Empire. They grew up in a culture heavily influenced by Greek ways. Greek was their mother-tongue. The population of Jews out in the Diaspora (or Dispersion—both are technical terms for the Jewish settlements beyond Palestine) was extensive. According to Philo, a Hellenistic Jewish author (20 B.C.E.–40 C.E.—roughly contemporaneous with Jesus), one million Jews were living in Alexandria, Egypt and another million were in the Roman provinces of Asia and Syria. One hundred thousand Jews lived in Italy.

Christian Jews preaching to non-Christian Hellenistic Jews could still assume that their hearers knew Jewish customs, traditions, and beliefs. They also had to assume awareness of some Greek and Roman customs and traditions. To be persuasive they had to adjust the style of their preaching and the manner of their behavior to accommodate themselves to a Judaism that had been even more strongly influenced by Hellenistic culture than had Palestinian Aramaic-speaking Judaism.

Equally significant for our understanding of the development of the Christian tradition is the recognition that in this stage of the spread of Christianity, the Hellenistic Jewish stage,[6] teaching and preaching were done in Greek. That required the translation of Aramaic stories about Jesus into Greek if they were to be useful in explaining the gospel to people who spoke Greek.

Translation from one language to another is a very difficult task. Few people do it well; no one translates faultlessly. It is rarely possible to find an exact one-to-one correlation between words in two different languages. Nuances shift. Imprecisions creep in. Word-plays and double meanings are obscured. Linguistic approximations occur. Something always gets lost in translation. When the translation occurs in an oral situation on the spur of the moment in response to a question, the difference between the original and its counterpart in the new language tends to be greater.

Underlying the factor of language difference were the differences in cultures. The Near-East Semitic culture of Palestine and the Hellenistic influences of the Greco-Roman culture, while not totally isolated from each other, were nevertheless quite different. Different modes of expression, different worldviews, different ways of thinking, different philosophical presuppositions all made the communications from one culture to the other difficult.

Christianity experienced a shift into yet a third stage. Christian preaching in the population centers of the Greco-Roman world, though persuading some Hellenistic Jews, began to attract large numbers of Gentiles. Christians became convinced that God was turning their attention away from the Jews and toward non-Jews. Consequently Christian preachers placed more emphasis on belief in Jesus as Christ (Messiah), and emphasized less the traditional Jewish religious practices. Strict observance of the requirements of Jewish law, celebrations of traditional Jewish holidays, and participation in the cultic sacrifices offered in the Temple in Jerusalem were stressed less. The more this tendency increased the less interested Jews were in Christian preaching.

The gap between Christianity and Judaism began to widen. As Jewish disenchantment increased so did Gentile interest. Soon Christianity was directing its preaching primarily to Gentile listeners. The relationship between Judaism and Christianity became strained and tense. The membership of the Christian church turned more and more Gentile.

The Apostle Paul, (the author of several "books"—actually, letters—in the New Testament, including Romans, 1 & 2 Corinthians and others), played a large role in the shift of early Christianity to the third stage. Presumably Paul himself was a Hellenistic Jew. Certainly he was a Jew. He did not call himself a Hellenist in his letters but his skill at writing in Greek strongly suggests that that language was his mother-tongue. Paul's letters clearly reflect his conviction that God, through his Holy Spirit, was using Paul to preach the gospel to non-Jews.[7] He believed that this was a divinely directed expansion of the Christian movement.

This third stage in the expansion of Christianity, the Hellenistic Gentile stage, turned the church toward the Gentiles. They were to become the primary source for the subsequent growth of Christianity. The missionary work of the church among the Jews, which had slowed, was soon to suffer a fatal set-back. Jewish Zealots, militant nationalistic Jews, fomented revolt against the Roman Empire. During the war that followed, the Roman armies devastated Jerusalem and destroyed the Temple in 70 C.E. The remnants of the Jewish Christian community in Jerusalem fled. Some fragments settled in Pella, a small town in the hills east of the Jordan River, but they were on the fringe of Christian expansion from then on.

This signaled the end for all practical purposes of Christian preaching to Aramaic-speaking Jews. Around the same time Hellenistic Jews came more and more to regard Christianity as a destructive rival of Judaism to be hated and opposed. Hostile antagonism toward Christians replaced the indifference with which most Hellenistic Jews had previously received Christian preaching. The church preached the gospel message primarily to the non-Jewish peoples of the Greco-Roman world after 70 C.E.

In this third, Hellenistic Gentile, stage of Christian expansion Christian preachers could not count on as thorough a familiarity with Jewish religious traditions from non-Jews as had been the case with Jews. They also had to cope with suspicion from misinformed minor Roman officials who regarded Christianity either as another type of

Jewish revolutionary sect or as a new political movement challenging the might of Imperial Rome.

The influence of the wide variety of pagan religions posed serious problems. Gentile converts frequently were tempted to mix Christianity with pagan beliefs and practices. Ideas and symbols which were important in pagan, non-Christian religions distorted central features of the Christian faith when they were combined. For instance previous experience with religious meals that were part of pagan worship confused some new Christians about the meaning of their joining in the Christian observance of the Eucharist, the Lord's Supper.

The shifts which Christian preaching experienced from one language to another, from one culture to another, from one type of audience to another all took place rapidly. Remember that Paul, who was a central figure in the shift from the second, Hellenistic Jewish stage to the third, Hellenistic Gentile stage, preached from approximately 40 to 55 C.E. That was only about ten years after the death of Jesus and the formation of the Christian church.

The success with which Christianity negotiated those enormous adjustments testifies to the resilient vitality of the new messianic faith. Such extensive transference of religious meaning from one culture to another required extraordinary openness and understanding. It also took considerable skill to adapt religious practices and traditions forged in one culture (the Semitic) to conform to the ways people thought and the symbols which were meaningful in another (Hellenistic) culture. The process modified the stories about Jesus which Christians used to explain their preaching and teaching.

We will examine several examples of this modification of stories about Jesus later. But by way of illustration let us consider one obviously modified Jesus tradition now.

The early church remembered that Jesus characteristically referred to God as "Father." As the form of address in prayer he taught the disciples to say "my father" or "our father." Jesus was a Palestinian Jew who spoke Aramaic. Apparently the Aramaic word he used was "abba." That is an unusual word to use with reference to God. It is the term a small child would use to a parent. A rough English equivalent would be "Daddy." A religious Jew would be very reluctant to address God in such a familiar, casual way.

The earliest Christians, being themselves Aramaic-speaking Jews, were impressed by the singularity of the term. They appreciated the new insight which it expressed into the intimate relationship with God they enjoyed because of their faith. They used it so frequently in their worship that it became a "fixed" term in Christian liturgy.

When Christianity moved into Greek-speaking areas the Aramaic word "abba" was unclear. So Christian preachers had to translate the term into Greek. We find Paul doing just that for the Greek-speaking readers of his letters (Rom. 8:15; Gal. 4:6). Even when a story about Jesus was told to Greek hearers a translation was necessary (cf. Mark 14:36). Sometimes the Aramaic term was omitted since it was obscure anyway (cf. Luke 22:42).

But the translation is inaccurate in that "abba" and the Greek term for father, "patēr," are not identical. The Greek word simply did not convey the same sense of intimate familiarity that the Aramaic term did. Matthew's translation, "my Father," (Matt. 26:39, 42) is closer than Luke's abrupt "Father" (Luke 22:42), but still it is inadequate.

The Gospel of John testifies further to the difference in the two words for "father." The Greek word is neutral enough that it can be used to refer to the devil (John 8:44). It is very unlikely that anyone whose mother-tongue was Aramaic would have used "abba" in that way. Probably a different Aramaic word lay behind John's tradition.

The Aramaic word "abba" appears very seldom in the Gospels. Yet surely we are not wrong in suspecting that it is the term behind many of the large number of times Jesus is described as calling God, "Father." And that is so in spite of the fact that the Greek word imprecisely represents the meaning of the Aramaic word. When an inexact Greek translation of an Aramaic word is itself translated into yet a third language (which is what has occurred with every one of our English versions) the potential for imprecision increases.

B. Preaching in an Oral Culture

The Gospels in the New Testament are, of course, written documents. We take it for granted that the easiest way to preserve and pass traditions on is to write them down. We thereby run the risk of overlooking the fact that the first century, C.E. had a civilization much different from ours. It was predominantly an oral culture.

Most people in the first century could not read or write. Only a small fraction of the population used written forms of communication. Those who could usually lived in the cultural and governmental centers of the empire such as Ephesus, Athens, Corinth, Alexandria, Jerusalem and, of course, Rome. Most of the people communicated with each other vocally rather than by writing.

Things are different today. Ours is basically a visual culture. The rate of literacy is relatively high. Much modern communication occurs through books, newspapers, magazines, and letters. Television and movies tell our stories.

We assume that a visual culture is better than an oral culture. Certainly there are great advantages. But people in an oral culture are aware of some features of oral tradition which visually oriented people sometimes miss. They know to listen for word-plays. They are alert for the sequence of events and the repetition of events in narrative recitation. Instinctively they hear the interplay of ideas and motifs. Brief allusions to other traditions cause them to recall unmentioned details of those traditions and relate them to the story being told. People of the first century world had learned to listen like that.

Early Christians were no exception. A few of them could read and write but most could not. Of course, spoken words were the means by which Christians preached and taught. When the need arose to explain some part of their preaching they told stories about Jesus which had been told to them by other Christians.

Both Jews and Christians yearned to know the sacred writings, the Jewish Scriptures. Most of them depended for instruction in those writings on the few in their communities who could read and interpret them.

The rabbis, the Jewish scholars, trained their students to commit to memory large portions of the Scriptures. They also learned by heart collections of rabbinical interpretation of the Scriptures. They were able to quote and appeal to these rabbinical opinions in disputes or to explain an interpretation. The first Christians, the Jewish Christians of Aramaic speaking Palestine, committed to memory and passed on the teachings and stories of Jesus in a similar way.

The discipline of memorization, so common in an oral culture but so painful for visual cultures like ours, continued to serve the church as it expanded beyond Palestine into the Hellenistic world. People were used to it and enjoyed memorization. And it's just as well. Books were very expensive to publish then. There were no mechanical printing presses. Books were composed by hand on hand-made paper. If other copies of a work were desired they had to be copied painstakingly by hand.

The first Christians were not interested in going to all that trouble and expense. Only a few of them could read. Oral preaching accompanied by stories of Jesus worked well. Besides, they all believed God was going to send Jesus back again and bring the world to an end soon. There was not time to waste writing books since there would be no need for books in just a little while.

Yet in spite of all those considerations we find the church only some thirty-five to forty years after its formation producing extended written accounts of the life of Jesus. Why did they do that? What led them to overcome the inertia of an oral culture (not to mention the expense of publishing)? There had to be compelling causes. Though we will consider those causes in more detail later, at least two might be mentioned here. First, Christians came to be not so convinced as they had been that Jesus was going to return right away. Second, the oral recounting of the Jesus traditions was not working as well as it once had. Stories about Jesus which once had explained aspects of the gospel message were, instead, obscuring it. As a consequence the church had much at stake in preserving the Jesus stories and restoring their capability for explaining gospel preaching.

C. Oral Traditions

Oral cultures develop patterns or forms with which they preserve and pass on those traditions which are significant to the culture. Ordinarily the patterns of oral tradition are brief "units" or story-forms that are easy to remember. The kinds of occasions for which the traditions have proven themselves meaningful influence the pattern of the forms in which the traditions are remembered. Occasions which shaped distinctive forms were funerals, weddings, coronations, victories, defeats, planting and harvest celebrations, worship, instruction, and so on.

Of course visual, literary cultures such as our own develop forms also. Since the forms can be captured and preserved by writing them down they tend to be longer and more complicated. We readily recognize the characteristic forms of wedding invitations, funeral notices, obituaries, TV soap ads, Thanksgiving hymns, even (the apex of confusing complexity) income tax forms.

The occasion or purpose for which the communication is intended shapes the kind of account which we write. By way of illustration Willi Marxsen reminds us that a person who has been involved in an automobile accident will describe the same event in three distinctively different ways: (1) to report it to the police, (2) to describe it in a letter to a friend, and (3) to record it in a private diary.[8] A description of the assassination of Martin Luther King, Jr. in a book on the history of the civil rights movement will differ considerably from a description of the same tragic event given at a human rights rally, or as an illustration in a sermon.

Since the early church originated and existed in an oral culture it also employed patterns or forms for remembering and passing on stories about Jesus. We have access to those forms of oral tradition only through the New Testament Gospels. Those are written documents which both included and also sometimes adapted stories about Jesus from the oral tradition to fit their purposes. But much had already taken place in early Christianity before the Gospels were written.

We have to assume that most of the stories of Jesus were first told by the Jewish Christians who belonged to the church in Palestine. They told the stories of Jesus in Aramaic. Before they were written down in our Gospels, however, Christianity had changed its direction of growth and was mainly a Greek-speaking Gentile oriented church. The stories of Jesus not only were translated from Aramaic to Greek but also were translated from a Semitic to a Hellenistic cultural context.

Now we must recognize another consideration which complicates our understanding of the history of the stories of Jesus even more. In the early church there was not one "theology" or set of beliefs about

Jesus which every Christian accepted. There were multiple "theologies" within early Christianity. It took years of conversation and reflection before a consensus of acceptance on some particular beliefs could be defined. Such a pluralism of theological views affected the church's uses of the Jesus stories. The story of the cleansing of the Temple (Mark 11:15–19) meant one thing if you thought Jesus was a prophet like the great prophets of the Jewish Scriptures (it meant he was trying to restore purity to Jewish religious worship). However, it meant something quite different if you believed Jesus was the Messiah (he was preparing the outer Temple area for the peoples of all nations who were to come streaming to Zion at the end of the world).

Yet a third complicating consideration must be taken into account. The early church used the stories of Jesus with great freedom. The same Jesus story could well be useful in a number of different settings. The account of his baptism (Mark 1:9–11) not only helped clarify the divine source of Jesus' lordly authority; it was also useful in instructing new converts about the meaning of baptism. It was appropriate to include in a service of baptism. It helped explain the church's belief that Christians also received the Holy Spirit at baptism. (Note that the church uses this story in all of these ways today, too.) In addition the early church used the story in its struggles with a competitive sect made up of the followers of John the Baptist. That accounts for some of the differences in Matthew's version compared with Mark's (cf. Matt. 3:13–17). The conflict with John the Baptist believers is even more evident in the Fourth Gospel (John 1:24–34).

The purposes for which the church found the stories of Jesus to be useful and meaningful molded its memory of those stories. The conviction of the first Christians that Jesus was the Messiah sent by God colored the stories about Jesus which they told. At any given moment in early Christianity it was the condition of the contemporary Christian community and the challenges it was facing at that time which determined the context from which Jesus was viewed and to which the Jesus tradition was adapted. Günther Bornkamm observes that "the particular situation of the community, its specific traditions, views, and modes of thought in various places, had a strong effect on the Jesus tradition. . . . The community incorporated its own experiences, questions, and insights into the tradition."[9]

The forces we have just been considering which affected the transmission of the stories about Jesus are not sufficient grounds for extreme skepticism about the accuracy of the Jesus stories. The conservatism of the earliest Jewish Christian disciples played a role in protecting the stories from radical change. The endurance of easily remembered oral forms also retarded tendencies to alter the stories.

But we do have to raise the question with each Jesus tradition whether that story reflects influences that came out of the life settings of early Christianity. In the stories of Jesus which have been preserved for us in the Gospels there is an intermingling of valued remembrances with the impact of the situation of the community which has remembered the stories for specific purposes. The result is an original blend of recollection and witness, of narrative and confession.

III. FORMS OF ORAL TRADITIONS

A. Form Criticism

We saw earlier that oral cultures developed brief, easily remembered forms or patterns for transmitting meaningful traditions. The purposes for which the traditions were remembered shaped the forms in which they were passed on. When several traditions were remembered for the sake of the same kind of occasion or purpose their forms were similar. By examining a number of examples one can discover the form common to all of them. Any other tradition which betrays that same form may be suspected to have been handed on for the same occasion or purpose.

In the nineteenth century scholars began to recognize the similarities in oral traditions and to define the forms or patterns by which they were passed on. This method of study was first applied not to the Bible but to Germanic and Scandinavian folk lore and fairy tales. Hermann Gunkel, a famous German Old Testament scholar, applied this method, which we now call "form criticism," to his studies of the traditions in Genesis in a book entitled *The Legends of Genesis,* published in German in 1901.

Encouraged by Gunkel's brilliant success three other German scholars adapted the method to study the oral traditions included in the New Testament Gospels. Karl Ludwig Schmidt and his teacher, Martin Dibelius (who gave the method its German name, "formge-schichte," or, "form criticism"), both published books in 1919 that launched the form critical study of the New Testament. Two years later Rudolf Bultmann's book *The History of the Synoptic Tradition* appeared. It was a very detailed attempt to classify all of the stories of Jesus in the first three Gospels according to categories of their forms or patterns. Form criticism of the New Testament had come into its own. In succeeding years, it has made a great contribution in helping us understand the traditions in the Gospels.[10]

Some people are alarmed by the use of the term "criticism" with a method of biblical study. But alarm is unnecessary. It's true that "criticism" can express the idea of severe judgment or censure, or even fault-finding. But the term can also be used to refer to any of a variety of methods of studying literary documents to understand them better. It is in this latter sense that the word is being used in the term "form criticism."

Form criticism as a method of literary study of the Gospels seeks to sort out the stories about Jesus and classify them according to their oral forms. It tries to identify the concern or purpose or situation which led early Christians to cast a tradition in a particular form. It also seeks to reconstruct the previous history of a story as an oral tradition before it was fixed as part of a written Gospel narrative. So then it raises the question as to the probable historical accuracy of a tradition. Did Jesus really say or do what the story says he did? Or was an insight out of early Christianity enshrined in an artificial "story of Jesus" context?

In the years since form criticism was first applied to the traditions in the Gospels its success at accomplishing its tasks has been varied. Its greatest achievements have been in the identification and classification of forms. Form critical scholars have found less unanimity when they have tried to describe what occasions produced each form.

Form criticism has been least successful in its attempts to trace the prior oral history of the Jesus traditions. This is because the process of oral transmission was complex. Only incomplete traces of that process have been preserved in the material of our Gospels. We are rarely able to reconstruct the previous stages with certainty.

When form critical scholars tried to determine the historical accuracy of the Jesus traditions they moved beyond the capabilities of form criticism as a method of literary analysis. Form criticism helps us identify the pattern by which the early church handed on meaningful traditions. It does not provide us with the kind of information which we need to make judgments about historical accuracy. Such evidence would include eyewitness testimony, pictures or sound-recordings of the event, corroborating descriptions from disinterested observers, and so on. Once the form of a tradition has been described, that tells us nothing about whether the event which the tradition relates really happened. As W. D. Davies appropriately observed, "the forms of sayings and stories in the Gospels do not decide their authenticity or historicity."[11]

In spite of those limits to what form criticism can do, some scholars have been very skeptical about the historical accuracy of any of the stories about Jesus. (Bultmann has been popularly included with these extreme skeptics, but that is not so.) Extreme suspicion simply is not justified. It is far more likely that the disciples reverently remembered and accurately reported their recollections of Jesus.

Nevertheless early Christians undoubtedly did crystallize some of their own experiences and insights into "story-of-Jesus" oral traditions. An example is the advice about how to cope with a sinning member of the community in Matthew 18:15–17. This is presented as a teaching from Jesus before his crucifixion. Yet it clearly presupposes that the church, which did not emerge until after his crucifixion and resurrection, has been in existence long enough to have struggled with the problem of how to discipline with love.

When early Christians created such a Jesus tradition they did not intend to deceive anyone. They believed that Jesus was alive and ruling in their midst. When, after struggle, worry and prayer, they defined a process for discipline, they believed it to be the Lord Jesus' spirit-inspired solution to their need. It genuinely was a word of Jesus. Only it was not a word that he had spoken during his Judean ministry but a word he spoke later to the Christian church. As a brief, oral form, that saying probably included no indication at all of when Jesus said it. Matthew may well have been the one responsible for placing it in a pre-crucifixion setting.

On the other hand, some stories of Jesus which were based on real events out of his life were so molded by theological or practical interests in the early church that we cannot recover their original setting. The varied versions of his birth clearly illustrate that. If we have trouble distinguishing with absolute certainty between traditions based on events in Jesus' life and traditions originating in the early church that does not make the first (and certainly by far the largest) group of traditions historically less accurate. The problem is not with the nature of the Jesus traditions. The problem lies with the limitations and inadequacies of the methodological tools we use to analyze them. Biblical scholarship constantly strives to improve its skills. Probably ten or fifty or a hundred years from now we will do better.

B. Classifications of Forms

It is surprising how many different Jesus traditions have similar forms. We have known about "parables" as an easily recognizable group of Jesus sayings for a long time. Although we talk frequently of the miracles of Jesus perhaps we have not realized that most of them follow a similar pattern. As we become more aware of the forms of the stories about Jesus that helps us more easily to see what the meaning of the tradition was. We learn to look beyond superficial details to the central significance which the early church saw in the story. It is that significance which caused the early church to value the story, mold it into an oral form and pass it on.

As we identify the forms we are pushing back behind the stage of the composition of the Gospels as documents. We hear again the stories of Jesus as separate individual accounts much as Christians heard them and used them during the first decades of the life of the church.[12]

1. The Pronouncement Story

The first category of the oral forms of the Jesus traditions is that of the *pronouncement story*. Some scholars have suggested other terms for this category, so we find these forms referred to sometimes as paradigms, apothegms, pronouncement sayings, anecdotes.

These stories are grouped together into the same category because they always contain a significant saying or pronouncement of Jesus. This is their most distinguishing characteristic They also have a distinctive structure or pattern—their "form." The structure includes a setting, an action (or brief dialogue), and a significant saying of Jesus. Some pronouncement story forms in our Gospels are fragmentary. They were sometimes shortened and accomodated to other traditional material by the Gospel writers or others.

When the full form is present it is self-contained with an identifiable beginning and ending. Usually there is no necessary connection to the material which precedes or follows it in the narrative of the Gospel. We can easily imagine its being used separately, by itself, as an isolated "unit" of oral tradition. At one time in the life of the church Christians told it as an independent story of Jesus.

The purpose of the pronouncement story form is to supply a brief narrative context for an important saying of Jesus. The function of the form is to furnish an anecdotal frame which serves to concentrate attention on the significant saying. Accordingly the setting is sparse and contains few details. Time references are general, places are vague, people are anonymous. It simply gives the irreducible minimum to provide an enhancing context for the saying.

Mark 2:15–17 is an example of a pronouncement story. We will divide it according to the parts of the pronouncement story form.

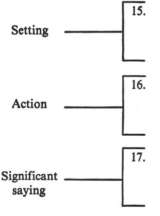

Setting	15.	And as he sat at table in his house, many tax collectors and sinners were sitting with Jesus and his disciples; for there were many who followed him.
Action	16.	And the scribes of the Pharisees, when they saw that he was eating with sinners and tax collectors, said to his disciples, "Why does he eat with tax collectors and sinners?"
Significant saying	17.	And when Jesus heard it, he said to them, "Those who are well have no need of a physician, but those who are sick; I came not to call the righteous, but sinners."

The scant detail in the setting is obvious. The only internal indication of chronology is the implication that it was mealtime. The place is Jesus' house, but the location is not described. There are classes of people present (tax collectors, sinners, disciples, scribes), but no names are given. The focus of the tradition is directed toward the memorable saying of verse 17.

Sometimes a saying of Jesus which was handed on in a pronouncement story form was expanded and interpreted by the early church. So, in this example, verse 17b: "I came not to call the righteous, but sinners" is an expansion which makes explicit the intent of verse 17a: "Those who are well have no need of a physician, but those who are sick."[13]

In Mark's version the narrative connectors which tie this tradition into the flow of his narrative are vague and indefinite. It was joined to the preceding material by the colorless "and." The tradition which follows the pronouncement story was connected to it with the vague word "now." Apparently Mark included the pronouncement story here because it referred to tax collectors, and he had just finished relating the call to discipleship of Levi, a tax collector (Mark 2:13–14). Luke improved the narrative connection (as he does frequently) by identifying Levi as the host of the dinner mentioned in the pronouncement story (Luke 5:29). What he did was useful, though, only when the two traditions were joined together in an extended narrative. When the traditions were independent oral units no connectives at all were necessary.

The tradition which Mark put after the pronouncement story, a dispute about fasting (Mark 2:18–22), was joined to it because both describe controversies between Jesus and those critical of his behavior. Again Luke sought to tie it more securely into that point in his narrative by changing the identity of the accusers from Mark's indefinite "people" (Mark 2:18) to "Pharisees," the same ones who had criticized Jesus in the pronouncement story (Luke 5:33; cf. vs. 30). Matthew wanted to make it more specific, too, so he identified the questioners as disciples of John the Baptist (Matt. 9:14), but did nothing to improve the narrative flow.

The entire tradition in its earliest, Markan version is self-contained and could easily be located at almost any point in the Gospel narrative.

Rudolf Bultmann divided this category of pronouncement stories further into three sub-sections: instructional stories (a saying addressed to disciples; an example is Luke 7:18–23), conflict stories (a saying addressed in response to an accusation or attack; another example besides the one just examined above is Mark 12:14–17), and biographical pronouncement stories (a saying called forth by an incident rather than by a question or a charge; examples are Mark 10: 13–16 and Mark 12:41–44).

His subdivisions do not modify our definition of the basic form of this type of oral tradition. They do provide an additional refinement in the classification of the form by grouping pronouncement stories according to the type of setting or interaction which introduces the significant saying. Scholars have identified about thirty-five stories of Jesus in the Gospels which exhibit the pronouncement story form we have just described.[14]

The early church cast sayings of Jesus into the pronouncement story form to illustrate and illumine problems which Christians were facing in their missionary preaching, in their corporate community life, and in their personal spiritual struggles. Pronouncement stories were mainly intended to facilitate missionary preaching but were also used for catechetical instruction. The conflict stories may also have been used by early Christians in their controversies with those who criticized and opposed the Christian faith.

2. The Miracle Story

A second category of oral tradition forms is the *miracle story.* "Novellen" or "tales" are other terms scholars have used to refer to this category.

The structure of the miracle story includes the description of the need, the miraculous act, and the results of the miracle. The results of the miracle may be represented by mention of its effect and/or of a response. The typical effects of miracle stories are (1) the cure of a disease in a healing miracle, (2) the restoration to life in a resuscitation miracle (when Jesus returns someone to life from death), (3) creation of order and plenty in a nature miracle (such as the stilling of the storm—Mark 4:35–41, or the feeding of the five thousand—Mark 6:30–44), (4) the departure of the demon in exorcism miracles. Responses to the miracle may come from the recipient(s) of the miracle, or from those observing the miracle, or from both.

The interest of the miracle story is not in something that Jesus said but in something that he did. It is an oral form designed to focus attention on a significant act. The act is a mighty deed which clearly discloses the supernatural power that Jesus possessed.

Let us see the structure of the miracle story form as it is reflected in Mark's account of the healing of Peter's wife's mother (Mark 1:29–31).

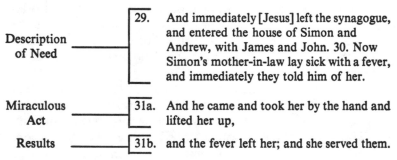

Description of Need

29. And immediately [Jesus] left the synagogue, and entered the house of Simon and Andrew, with James and John. 30. Now Simon's mother-in-law lay sick with a fever, and immediately they told him of her.

Miraculous Act

31a. And he came and took her by the hand and lifted her up,

Results

31b. and the fever left her; and she served them.

In this example the first part of verse 29 serves as a narrative connector. "And immediately [Jesus] left the synagogue and entered the house . . ." ties this tradition to the preceding episode in Mark's narrative, Jesus' healing of a possessed man in the synagogue at Capernaum (Mark 1:21–28). Mark probably added the connector to help the sequential flow of his narrative. We may speculate that in its oral form as a self-contained, independent unit of tradition the story began with a simple introduction something like "One day Jesus was in the house of Simon. . . ."

Verse 30 describes what the problem is and gets that information to Jesus. The first half of verse 31 brings Jesus to Peter's mother-in-law where he does the mighty act, he lifts her up. The rest of verse 31 describes the results of the miraculous act which includes both the effect ("the fever left her") and a response ("she served them").

Although the brevity of this miracle story exposes the essential structure of the form more clearly its conciseness is not typical of the miracle story form. Unlike the terse pronouncement story the miracle story frequently is embellished with extensive detail. There is usually not the same minimal detail as in the first form we discussed. Extended conversation between Jesus and the affected persons, or with those who brought them, or with the disciples usually occurs. The miraculous act may be accomplished by a word of power or a healing gesture such as a touch or the taking of the hand (as in our example) or the application of mud. The healing of the Gerasene demoniac (Mark 5:1–20) or the healing of the boy with epilepsy (Mark 9:17–29) illustrate this tendency toward elaboration of detail.

Early Christians soon became interested in embellishing and novelizing Jesus traditions. Popular Christianity told the stories of Jesus not just to teach a lesson. They took pleasure in the narrative for its own sake. They let their imaginations supply details, expand on brief allusions to people and events, and "fill in the gaps" they found in the stories about Jesus they had heard. They did the same thing with stories about events and important people in the beginning years of the life of the church.[15]

Now we must make an observation which at first may seem confusing. It is important to remember that "miracle story" as a form-critical category is a description of one class of the oral, pre-literary forms of the Jesus traditions. Form-critical categories are not primarily governed by the content of the tradition. So some Jesus traditions which clearly describe miraculous happenings are classified as "pronouncement stories" by form criticism. This is because they were told by early Christians to direct attention to a saying of Jesus rather than to a miraculous act. The healings of the Syrophoenician woman's daughter (Mark 7:25–30) and of the centurion's servant (Matt. 8:5–13) are two examples of this phenomenon.

Scholars have further sub-divided the category of the miracle story according to the kinds of miraculous deeds the stories recount. Names and examples of the sub-divisions of the miracle story category include exorcisms (Mark 1:23–28), healings (Mark 1:29–31), resuscitations (Luke 7:11–17), and nature miracles (Mark 4:35–41).

Early Christians valued and retold the miracle stories because they dramatically supported Christian preaching and teaching by showing

Jesus as one who had access to the supernatural power which represented the presence of the kingly rule of God. The function of the miracle stories was to portray Jesus as the Messiah, who was far superior to any of the miracle working figures in the Jewish religious traditions. Of course the Jewish Scriptures portray major figures in Israel's history, such as Moses, Samuel, Elijah, Elisha, and several of the prophets, doing miraculous acts. It is interesting to note that many of those miracle stories have the same structure as the miracle stories of Jesus. Look, for instance, at the Elijah miracle story in 1 Kings 17:17–24. The rabbinical traditions also contain accounts of famous rabbis who were capable of accomplishing miracles.

We have described only two form critical categories of the Jesus stories. But before we go on, let's look at a story of Jesus in the Gospels which has some of the structural features of both the pronouncement story and the miracle story. This gives us some inkling of the tremendous assistance which the definition by form critical scholars of categories of the oral tradition has provided for study of the Jesus traditions in the Gospels. The story we will consider is the healing of the paralytic (Mark 2:1–12).[16] This pericope (selection or passage, from the Greek, meaning "to cut around, away") does not conform to the structures of either the miracle story or the pronouncement story.

There are, however, some phrases in the story as it now appears in Mark's Gospel which we may bracket and set aside as having probably been added by Mark. They would therefore not have been part of the story when it was being told as an independent unit of tradition. Verses 1–2 are likely a Markan editorial expansion of the beginning of the tradition which probably reported simply that Jesus was in a house. With these verses Mark provided editorial linkage which connected this tradition into the flow of his narrative sequence: "And when he returned to Capernaum after some days. . . ." In verses 3–4 Mark also explained (albeit inexactly[17]) for his Hellenistic Gentile audience why the paralytic was let down through the roof: crowds were blocking all other avenues of access. In its oral form the story may only have reported that some men lowered a paralytic through the roof into Jesus' presence.

Verses 5b–10 turn the account in a new and different direction. If they are regarded as an interpolation (a later addition) and removed, what remains perfectly reflects the form of the miracle story as we have defined it. A paralytic is brought by his friends into a house where Jesus was (the description of need). Jesus told the paralytic to get up, pick up his pallet and walk (the miraculous act). The man did what he was told and the observers were amazed and glorified God (the results, including both the effect and the response).

The section which we tentatively removed as a possible addition (vss. 5b–10) has the appearance of a fragment of a pronouncement story. When the story circulated independently it emphasized a Jesus saying concerning his authority to forgive sins. Whoever incorporated this pronouncement story into the miracle story changed it to meld smoothly with the other tradition by dropping the beginning and ending. Although Mark could have combined the two traditions himself it is equally possible that they were already combined at some time prior to the composition of his Gospel. It is very likely that at one time both stories circulated as independent, self-contained units of Jesus tradition.

The story of the healing of the paralytic is not an isolated instance. Early Christians often modified stories of Jesus. Such accommodation and adaptation occurred frequently in the early church as it applied the units of the Jesus tradition to varied and changing circumstances. For example the same significant saying of Jesus has been provided two different anecdotal settings in Luke (Luke 8:19–21 and 11:27–28; compare Mark 3:31–35 and Matt. 12:46–50).

3. Stories About Christ

A third category for the classification of the oral forms of the Jesus tradition is "stories about Christ." Since these traditions have a strong christological thrust, that is a more accurate designation than "stories about Jesus" which has also been suggested. Form critical scholars have also referred to this group as myths and legends. Some attempts have been made to divide this category into sub-divisions of "legend" and "myth" but this distinction has not won wide acceptance.

Terminology such as "legend" and "myth" can be problematic. People frequently use these terms wrongly to convey the idea of fraudulent and pious fantasy. But form criticism does not use these terms in this popular but inaccurate and confusing sense.

"Legend" is a technical term of literary analysis which refers to stories about holy people and religious heroes. These stories are intended to be read (legend is derived from *legendus,* the gerund form of the Latin *legere* = to read) for inspiration, instruction, and spiritual edification. Medieval collections of lives of the saints were called "legende." To refer to a Jesus tradition as legend in this technical sense is not a negative judgment on its accuracy as historical reporting. Rather it is simply to describe this particular tradition as having been fixed in oral form and passed on by early Christians because of its usefulness for inspiration and edification.

"Myth" is also a technical term of literary criticism. Although it is popularly understood to imply that the content is fictitious or invented (almost a synonym with fable or fairy-tale) that is inexact and misleading. The technical meaning of "myth" is a narrative expression of an idea foundational to human existence which can be known, experienced, and appropriated repeatedly by way of recitation and ritual. To designate a unit of Jesus tradition as myth is not to assess its historicity. Rather it is to describe that narrative tradition as expressing an affirmation or concept which is fundamental to the distinctive mode of human existence called Christian.

The traditions which form criticism includes in this category are those stories which emphasize the identity of Jesus as the Christ of God. This would include the infancy narratives, the story of the twelve-year-old Jesus at the Temple, his baptism by John the Baptist, the temptation, the transfiguration, the triumphal entry into Jerusalem, and so on.

Some form-critical scholars place the Passion narrative, the account of Jesus' last days in Jerusalem including his arrest, trial, and crucifixion, in a special class by itself. For the purposes of this cursory overview of the classes of oral forms we will include it in "stories about Christ." There is general agreement among New Testament scholars that the Passion narrative existed from the earliest period of Christianity as a continuous narrative. It was the cardinal myth, in the sense in which we defined that term above, of the Christian faith. Nevertheless we should not suppose that the Passion narrative underwent no changes as it was handed on through the various stages of early Christianity. The divergences in the first three Gospels' accounts of Passion Week, Paul's description in 1 Corinthians 11 of the institution of the Lord's Supper independent of a full Passion narrative, and the absence of a similar tradition in the Passion narrative of the Gospel of John (although he certainly presupposes it) all confirm that modifications were made on parts of the Passion narrative, too.

The purpose for which this category of traditions was developed was to aid the cultic worship of the church. They enriched its rites and ceremonies. Obviously they were also employed for preaching purposes and as teaching aids. Because their meaning was so central for the Christian movement they were always liable to development and elaboration.

4. Sayings of the Lord

A fourth major form category into which the oral traditions about Jesus are classified is variously titled "sayings of Jesus," "*sayings of the Lord*" or "dominical sayings."[18]

This category is comprised of independent sayings of Jesus which have no narrative setting or framework. The sayings were transmitted in the oral tradition as isolated Jesus sayings or were grouped together in brief or more extended discourse fashion. It seems likely that some of the methods of arrangement of groups of these sayings as seen in the Gospels reflect the ways in which the sayings may have been clustered together in the oral tradition.

Sometimes the arrangement is artificial and is governed by "catchwords" or superficial similarity of content. In Mark 4:21–25 the sayings about the lamp and about the purpose of hiding (vss. 21–22) are related because both have to do with the ideas of concealment and disclosure of light. The two sayings in verses 24–25 are connected because of the common theme of gain and loss. The two groups of double sayings are joined apparently on the basis of the repetition of the admonition to "hear." That exhortation concludes the first group of double sayings, verse 23, and is echoed in the first saying of the second group, "Take heed what you *hear.* . . . " The second saying of the second group, verse 25, may be found in the Gospel of Matthew appended to the Parable of the Talents (Matt. 25:29). This suggests that at an earlier stage in primitive Christianity the saying was circulating as an independent, detached tradition. It was subsequently incorporated into the parable tradition by unknown early Christians. During the same period it was also added into a sayings group (see also Luke 19:26 and Matt. 13:12).

In Luke 6:27–38 we find a much more complex and integrated internal cohesiveness. This passage is composed of three groups of parallel sayings (vss. 27–30, 32–34, 37–38). Each group is related to a summary statement (vss. 31, 35, 36). All of the summaries express some aspect of the ethical principle of reciprocity. The whole section displays a sophisticatedly devised and carefully constructed internal order.

Since Jesus was a Jew, and the first Christians who passed his sayings on were Jews, these sayings of the Lord reflect many features which are characteristic of Hebrew poetic and rhetorical style. We can often observe rhythym and structured pattern.

The use of parallelism is typical of the Hebrew style. Jewish writers used four basic kinds of parallelism. When the second verse repeats the thought of the first while using other words, that is *synonymous* parallelism:

> "Do not be anxious about your life, what you shall eat,
> nor about your body, what you shall put on.
> For life is more than food,
> And the body more than clothing." (Luke 12:22–23)

In *antithetical* parallelism the second verse expresses the opposite thought of the first line:

> "Every sound tree bears good fruit,
> but the bad tree bears evil fruit.
> A sound tree cannot bear evil fruit,
> nor can a bad tree bear good fruit." (Matt. 7:17–18)

Synthetic parallelism has the second verse flowing as a continuing logical extension of the thought of the first verse:

> "They love the place of honor at feasts and the best seats in the synagogues,
> and salutations in the market places, and being called rabbi by men."
> (Matt. 23:6–7)

When the thought of the second line builds on and goes beyond the thought of the first line in a climactic manner the parallelism is *tautologic:*

> "He who receives you receives me,
> and he who receives me receives him who sent me." (Matt. 10:40)

Scholars have defined five sub-divisions for the "sayings of the Lord" category.

1. *Logia* (sing. = logon) or wisdom sayings are very similar to the Near-Eastern wisdom traditions collected in Jewish Wisdom Literature such as Proverbs, Ecclesiastes, and, in the intertestamental literature, The Wisdom of Solomon.

> "If a kingdom is divided against itself, that kingdom cannot stand. And if a house is divided against itself, that house will not be able to stand." (Mark 3:24–25)

Other examples are Mark 7:15; 9:50; 11:24–25; Matthew 6:23; Luke 6:27–31.

2. *Prophetic* and *apocalyptic sayings* are similar to the formulations of prophetic and apocalyptic literature in the Jewish Scriptures (Isaiah, Jeremiah, Ezekiel, Amos, Daniel, etc.). The prophetic literature depicted the prophet as the spirit-empowered agent of God who called Israel to faithfulness and warned of coming judgment for infidelity. Apocalyptic writings were a special kind of literature which expressed present occurrences and end-time expectations in visionary language.

> "But woe to you that are rich, for you have received your consolation. Woe to you that are full now, for you shall hunger. Woe to you that laugh now, for you shall mourn and weep." (Luke 6:24–25)

> "And brother will deliver up brother to death, and the father his child, and children will rise against parents and have them put to death; and you will be hated by all for my name's sake. But he who endures to the end will be saved." (Mark 13:12–13)

Additional examples are Matthew 23:13–39; 25:1–13; Luke 12:35–58; 21:34–36; Mark 13:1–2, 5–37.

3. Under the sub-category of *legal sayings* and *community rules* form critical scholars group those sayings of the Lord which require duties and offer guidelines for how individual Christians and the Christian church are to conduct their lives.

> "And whenever you stand praying, forgive, if you have anything against any one; so that your Father also who is in heaven may forgive you your trespasses." (Mark 11:25)

> "If your brother sins against you, go and tell him his fault, between you and him alone. If he listens to you, you have gained your brother. But if he does not listen, take one or two others along with you, that every word may be confirmed by the evidence of two or three witnesses. If he refuses to listen to them, tell it to the church; and if he refuses to listen even to the church, let him be to you as a Gentile and a tax collector." (Matt. 18:15–17)

More examples of this sub-category are Mark 3:28–29; 10:11–12; Matthew 5:17–48; 18:19–20; Luke 10:2–16.

4. A fourth sub-category is composed of the *"I" sayings* of Jesus or christological sayings. These are sayings attributed to Jesus in the oral tradition in which he claims some special identity or makes a demand for himself. A multiple example is:

> "I came to cast fire upon the earth; and would that it were already kindled! I have a baptism to be baptised with; and how I am constrained until it is accomplished! Do you think that I have come to give peace on earth? No, I tell you, but rather division . . ." (Luke 12:49–51)

Additional sayings of this type may be found in Matthew 5:17; 12:40; Mark 8:38; 9:41; Luke 9:23; 19:10.

5. A final group of Jesus sayings traditions which form criticism has described is the sub-division of *parable* with its related forms of metaphor, simile, and similitude.

A *metaphor* is the use of a concrete incident from common, everyday life to express an abstract concept:

> "No one sews a piece of unshrunk cloth on an old garment; if he does, the patch tears away from it, the new from the old, and a worse tear is made." (Mark 2:21)

The *simile* explicitly identifies the abstract concept and connects it to the figure with the word "like":

> "Woe to you [Pharisees]! for you are like graves which are not seen, and men walk over them without knowing it." (Luke 11:44)

The *similitude* expands the simile by adding detail:

> "Will any one of you, who has a servant plowing or keeping sheep, say to him when he has come in from the field, 'Come at once and sit down at table'? Will he not rather say to him, 'Prepare supper for me, and gird yourself and serve me, till I eat and drink; and afterward you shall eat and drink'? Does he thank the servant because he did what was commanded? So you also, when you have done all that is commanded of you, say, 'We are unworthy servants; we have only done what was our duty.'" (Luke 17:7–10)

The *parable* is a brief story which dramatizes a common human experience from which it draws its comparison or analogy. It commends itself to the hearers since they have experienced the circumstance which controls the analogy. The entire story is directed to a single, central point. When the point is grasped the parable has accomplished its didactic purpose. The rest of the detail is secondary in importance.[19] Luke 15:3–10 contains two parables both of which are based on the common human experience of losing (and the anxiety which results) and finding (resulting in joy). If we ignore the way a parable was intended to function when it was first told we may divert attention away from the single, central point by focusing too much attention on secondary details. When we do that we convert the parable into an allegory. Allegory is not analogical but rather finds hidden, special meaning in all details. Mark 4:13–20 gives an allegorical interpretation of the parable of the seed and the soils.

Related to the parable is the illustrative or exemplary story. This story differs from the parable in that, though it relates a concrete incident from life, it does not draw its analogy from a human experience common to the listeners. The story of the two prodigals (Luke 15:11–32) is an example of this type of story.

IV. THE HISTORY OF THE TRADITION

A. *Traces of the Past*

We have seen that the stories about Jesus which told of his words and works were originally cast into oral forms by early Christians and passed on verbally. Jewish Christians who spoke Aramaic were responsible for the first phases of this transmission process. But we know these stories of Jesus only through the New Testament Gospels. We have access to them only in the versions in which those stories have been adapted and assimilated into written, continuous, narrative prose. Furthermore, that prose was written in Greek.

In the interval between the first time those Jesus stories were told by Jewish Christians and the time when they were recorded in the Gospels by Gentile Christians a lot had happened. The language Christians used changed from Aramaic to Greek. The people who told the stories and the people who heard the stories shifted from Palestinian Jews to Hellenistic Jews and then on to Hellenistic Gentiles. In that complex process Christians changed details and accommodated the stories to new interests as the need arose. Often we cannot be certain what the exact form of a particular tradition was when it was first spoken. We simply do not know how to recover the original versions.

Before a story was recorded some development occurred in the complicated career of the oral tradition. We can still partially trace that growth in the versions of the traditions as they appear in the Gospel narratives. Sometimes the same Jesus word is available in two versions, one simple and the other complex (compare Matt. 10:24–25 with Luke 6:40). Sometimes questions are converted into statements (compare Mark 4:21 with Matt. 5:15, Luke 8:16 and 11:33). Sometimes additions are made (compare Luke 6:31 with Matt. 7:12, or Mark 6:7 with Luke 9:1–2). William Barclay gives an interesting example extending well into the second century which illustrates the growth and development of the Jesus traditions.[20]

> Mark 2:17: "I came not to call the righteous, but sinners."
>
> Luke 5:32: "I have not come to call the righteous, but sinners to repentance."

Justin Martyr, *Apology* 1:15: "I came not to call the righteous, but sinners to repentance, for the heavenly Father desires the repentance of the sinner rather than his punishment."

We should not be surprised that such changes took place in the transmission of the oral tradition. We can observe a similar process at work in the way in which the Gospel writers adapted the traditions they had received to their own purposes. Matthew and Luke freely reinterpreted Mark's Gospel, which was one source of the tradition for them.[21] It is only logical to assume that they reworked other written and oral tradition sources in a similar fashion. They were simply continuing a practice which the first Christians had begun.

B. Post-Ascension Jesus Traditons

The difficulties we face in retracing the history of the stories of Jesus are even more complicated. Sometimes what has been preserved as a Jesus tradition in the written Gospels actually is a community construction. That is to say, it was formulated by someone in the early church rather than remembered from the ministry of Jesus.

The first Christians were not dependent solely on the recollections and reminiscences of their associations with Jesus during the period of his public ministry. They firmly believed he was alive and was speaking to them and in them by his Spirit. They were bound together in fellowship with him and he was guiding and directing their lives. They identified the Jesus whom the eyewitnesses had known during his earthly career with the resurrected and exalted Lord who was speaking to them through his Spirit-filled prophets.

Christians make the same assumption of identity today. The saying, "Behold, I stand at the door and knock; if any one hears my voice and opens the door, I will come in to him and eat with him, and he with me" (Rev. 3:20) is a word of Jesus, and it is no less authoritative because it was not spoken by Jesus during his teaching ministry in Palestine. If ours were an oral culture and Jesus traditions were still being communicated verbally, that saying could easily become detached and transmitted as an independent word of the Lord. Then it could acquire a brief narrative setting. That would present it as a pronouncement story, which could appear to have had its origin in the public ministry of Jesus.

Another, different example will help illustrate this important point about the early church and the oral traditions. Two New Testament texts which sometimes are quoted as Jesus sayings, although they are not, are, "Love covers a multitude of sins" (1 Pet. 4:8) and "Do not let the sun go down on your anger" (Eph. 4:-26).[22] Early Christians in an oral culture would be inclined to identify those admonitions as being equally as inspired by the Spirit of the Lord as the sayings Jesus uttered during his preaching ministry. Only because copies of the documents in which these sayings were originally written have been preserved is it possible for us to correct the erroneous popular identification of them as words of Jesus. Yet in one sense they are his words, but only in an extended, theological sense. They do not contain historical reminiscences of the earthly Jesus.

When the early Christians expanded, interpreted, reapplied, and adapted the Jesus traditions they did not intend to confuse or deceive anyone. Although they changed the stories they were faithful to what they regarded as their Spirit-endowed perception of how those traditions interacted with their specific needs and problems. Even when they engaged in the Spirit-inspired formulation of new words of the Lord it was not intended as a subterfuge. It was a legitimate expression of their continuing response to the living Lord of the church.[23]

In the process of the transmission and development of the oral tradition it was neither practical, possible, or appropriate for the first Christians to maintain careful distinctions between Spirit-inspired community constructions and authentic historical reminiscence. It is unfair and insensitive for us to expect early Christians to have valued and passed on exactly those traditions which are of special interest to our contemporary curiosity. It is equally unfair for us to expect them to have preserved classifications of Jesus traditions governed by criteria which had not been defined until the post-Enlightenment development of modern historiography. Yet that is exactly what we demand when we want to know of a particular tradition, "Did Jesus really say (or, do) this?"

C. The Fixing of Oral Traditions

The authors of the Gospels in our New Testament drew heavily on the fund of anecdotes about Jesus which had been preserved in oral traditions. They used these stories as building blocks to construct written narratives spanning the entire career of Jesus. The oral traditions they used still retained some of their features as oral forms. They also frequently display evidence of some of the changes and adaptations that took place in the process of oral transmission.

The stories about Jesus were adapted yet once more. As the Gospel writers included the traditions in their narratives they also introduced changes. Some of the changes were literary changes. They were necessary to incorporate the story smoothly into the flow of the extended narrative. The evangelists introduced other changes so that the traditions in their Gospel narratives would explicitly support theological ideas they thought were important. They also made some alterations so that the stories of Jesus clearly spoke to the troublesome issues with which the evangelists' own communities were struggling.

Once these oral traditions were committed to writing they became relatively stabilized. They were "fixed" in written form, which is not nearly so susceptible to changes as verbal material is. Yet we need to note two qualifications registered against that observation. First, the oral stories continued to be used after the Gospels were written. They continued to be adapted to other new life situations and to develop concurrently with the use of the written Gospels. Second, the stabilization of the oral traditions in written form was not so rigid or immediately so sacrosanct that Matthew and Luke hesitated to change Mark. To that extent we must still reckon with continued change in the stories the church told about Jesus. That change stopped only when the four Gospels in our New Testament came to be regarded by the early church as authoritative and normative.

A major task which confronted Mark as the first evangelist was the construction of a continuous story out of the many single stories and brief blocks of Jesus traditions which were in circulation. He supplied indications of time and place which served as connectors. They provided the impression of consecutive ordering to his account. This achieved the fascinating literary advantage of presenting the unrelated traditions in a narrative sequence. It read like a continuous story. But this suggests that the sequence in the written narratives, except perhaps in the broadest, most general outline, is not a dependable resource for the reconstruction of the sequence of the events that really occurred in the career of Jesus. Since our Gospels are our only sources of information about his career we must reluctantly acknowledge that the real sequence of events cannot be recovered.

We must make another adjustment to our understanding of Mark's accomplishment as an author. Up until now the discussion has given the impression that until Mark composed his Gospel verbal modes were the only manner that Jesus traditions were available. Mark's task then would seem to be that of a good listener and collector who set down in writing the Jesus traditions for the first time. That impression is surely inaccurate.

Scholars believe that before Mark wrote his Gospel smaller collections of Jesus traditions had already been composed. They continued to exist concurrently with his Gospel. He may well have derived some of his traditions from such documents.

Where did they come from and why were they written? None of them has survived as separate documents. Scholars conjecture their existence because indications in our written Gospels seem to demand the supposition. We do not know who wrote them, or where they were written, or for whom they were written.

Some collections may have been composed to make certain stories of Jesus more readily available for early Christians to read in worship. Those readings at first supplemented and perhaps, eventually, replaced the readings from the Jewish Scriptures. Christians collected other traditions in brief tracts to serve as resources for Christian missionary preaching or catechetical instruction. "Testimonia" or short collections of citations from Jewish Scriptures were probably compiled to support the Christian conviction that many of the events in the life and ministry of Jesus were a fulfillment of ancient Israelite anticipations. Those are just some of the motives for gathering stories of Jesus which we can imagine. Since no collections have survived intact scholars are unable either to establish or disprove their existence. Nevertheless the conjecture of one such collection has proven to be exceptionally fruitful in the study of the Gospels as we will see in the next chapter.

V. THE GOSPEL AND THE GOSPELS

A. Meaning of "Gospel"

We have used the term "gospel" mainly to refer to a type of written document, such as the first four books of the New Testament. But this is really an extended meaning of the term. That use became prevalent in the church only during the latter part of the second century. The primary sense of "gospel" was "to proclaim good news." The term conveyed sacral meanings in first century Greek vocabulary because it was used in the Imperial cult (a Greco-Roman pagan religion which worshiped Caesar) to refer to the birth of an emperor-god.

More important for its use in early Christianity were the meanings adhering to the term from Jewish scriptural traditions which had been translated into Greek. "To bring good news" was used in the Jewish Scriptures to refer to the naming of a king (1 Kings 1:42), the birth of a son (Jer. 20:15), and victory in battle (1 Sam. 31:8–10). The servant songs of Isaiah celebrated the anticipation of the coming of the Servant of God who would "proclaim the good news" of deliverance and of the introduction of the new age, the restoration of the kingly rule of God (Isa. 40: 1–5; 52:7–10).

With this background the implications were very profound and far-reaching when early Christians used the term "gospel" to summarize the preaching of Jesus.

> Now after John was arrested, Jesus came into Galilee, preaching the *gospel* of God, and saying, "The time is fulfilled, and the kingdom of God is at hand; repent, and believe in the *gospel.*" (Mark 1:14–15; italics added)

Here it is clear that "gospel" does not mean a book nor even does it mean the life, death, and resurrection of Jesus. It means the announcement of the inbreaking of the new age of God's rule.

The early Christian community did not materially change the content of that announcement when, on the conviction of its Easter faith, Christians proclaimed *Jesus* as the mediator sent by God to establish that new age. But they broadened the term significantly. It referred specifically now to the death and resurrection of Jesus. The message of Jesus raised from the dead was "gospel." Words about Jesus as living savior were "gospel." To preach the gospel meant to testify that Jesus was the Messiah whom God had vindicated by raising him from the dead and through whom he was continuing to work salvifically. It was "good news" that in Jesus' death and resurrection the inbreaking of the new age of God's rule had begun.

The gospel of the early church focused primarily on the proclamation of the death and resurrection of Jesus. It urged the hearer to believe the claim of God. If the listener received it faithfully and trustingly, it accomplished salvation. This is the dominant sense in which Paul used the term "gospel." It occurs some sixty times in the literature of the Pauline corpus (see especially Rom. 1:1–5, 16; 1 Cor. 1:17–24; 15:1–5). But later Christian writers also frequently used it in this sense (see Mark 13:10; 14:9).

Mark, however, also used the term, "gospel," in another way.[24] He introduced his composition with the words, "the beginning of the *gospel* of Jesus Christ, the Son of God" (Mark 1:1, italics added). In that instance he used the term to refer not just to Jesus' death and resurrection, but to the entire public ministry of Jesus which culminated in the Passion narrative.

Mark shared Paul's conviction that the cross event was the central focus of the Easter faith. His use of the term "gospel" to refer to the whole of his narrative implied that in his view the earthly ministry traditions were to be understood in a subordinate position to the Passion narrative. What does that mean? Mark felt that the stories out of the ministry of Jesus were incomprehensible unless they were heard on the presupposition of the cross event, the crucifixion, and resurrection of Jesus. " 'The earthly work of Jesus is narrated as illustration of the message of Christ.' "[25] It may be identified with the term "gospel" in so far as it illumines and clarifies that central "gospel" content.

Mark was not disassociating the term "gospel" from the core content of the Easter proclamation. By redefining the boundaries of what the term encompassed he was refocusing the term and inviting further development. Others were quick to take advantage of that. So Matthew's phrase "the gospel of the kingdom" refers primarily to the collected teachings of Jesus (Matt. 4:23; 24:14). In Luke it is not Jesus' death but his life and ministry which provide the pattern for Christian discipleship. In his second volume, Acts, pivotal components of the ministry of Jesus were duplicated in the missionary careers of Peter and Paul.

It was not until the second century gave way to the third that we find the use of "gospel" as a designation for a book (Clement of Alexandria, *Stromata* I:136:1). Other evidence of the technical use of the term as a designation for a type of literature is found in the numerous apocryphal (literally "hidden," but then the word came to mean "non-canonical") gospels produced by second, third, and fourth century Christianity. These include such works as the Gospel of Thomas, the Gospel of Peter, the Gospel of Philip, the Gospel of the Egyptians, the Gospel of the Twelve, to name only a few.

We should note that when each of the canonical Gospels were written the author meant for his document to be used by itself, and not supplemented by other gospels. "The formation of the four-gospel Canon is an historical and theological development of the second century which was neither intended nor forseen by any of the Evangelists."[26]

B. The Synoptic Gospels

Most of what we have discussed in this chapter also has significance for the study of the Gospel of John. But that work will be ignored in the rest of this book except for incidental mention.

The Gospel of John stands in a class by itself. Its author was a highly creative theologian. It was produced among a group of early Christians which was quite different from the Christian communities for which the Gospels of Matthew, Mark, and Luke were written. It would not be inexact for us to think of John's community as a sort of sect of early Christians who were on the fringes of the Christianity that produced the first three Gospels.[27]

There is an interrelatedness between the first three Gospels that John does not share. That interrelatedness is due partly to similar theological views and beliefs. But it owes most to the literary dependancy of the three, as we will see later on. The similarity between the three is so pronounced that scholars have grouped Matthew, Mark, and Luke together as the "Synoptic" Gospels. They may be set side by side and "viewed together" (that's what "synoptic" means) in a comparative way. These Synoptic Gospels are the primary concern of this study.

C. Authorship Unknown

The early view of the church (second century at the earliest) held that the Gospel of Matthew was written by the former tax collector, Matthew Levi, who became one of the Twelve. At least it incorporated many traditions about Jesus which were ultimately dependent upon Matthew. The Gospel of Mark was written by John Mark who, after his associations with Paul, served as an assistant to Peter. Luke, the "divine physician" who was a companion of Paul, authored the Third Gospel. It now appears unlikely that any of these identifications are accurate. At any rate the data to verify those ancient traditions simply are not available.

We must candidly acknowledge that all three of the Synoptic Gospels are anonymous documents. None of the three gains any importance by association with those traditional figures out of the life of the early church. Neither do they lose anything in importance by being recognized to be anonymous. Throughout this book the traditional names are used to refer to the authors of the first three Gospels but we shall do so simply as a device of convenience.

CHAPTER TWO
Why Write a Gospel?
The Gospel of Mark

During the first decades of Christianity, Christians spread throughout the Roman Empire preaching their gospel. As they preached, their non-Christian listeners asked them questions about what they were saying. To clarify their preaching the Christians told stories of Jesus. Though they were not always successful that method seemed to work pretty well. Yet just a few short years later we find that the early church produced a considerable body of literature which has been expanding ever since. What caused those early Christians to turn to writing?

In this chapter we will consider the emergence of Christian writings in general, then, specifically, the composition of the Gospel of Mark. We will explore Mark's purposes, identify features that specially mark his Gospel, consider his identity, and review the contents of his work. Then we will broaden our perspective to consider the relationship of Mark's Gospel to the first and third Gospels, Matthew and Luke. That will lead us into a consideration of what scholars have come to call the "Q" source.

I. CHRISTIAN WRITINGS EMERGE

As we saw in the last chapter Christianity began in a culture which was predominantly oral. People ordinarily communicated with one another verbally. That being the case Christians were more inclined to pass the stories about Jesus on by word of mouth rather than to record them in writing.

Other factors helped to retard the production of documents about Jesus. Hand-written books composed on hand-made paper were very expensive to produce. So were duplicate volumes of the same work. Scribes tediously copied them by hand. During the early years of the church most Christians were convinced that Jesus was going to return from heaven in a very short while. They thought they were living in the last days of the present order. The world as we know it would shortly come to an end. They had more pressing work to do in the brief span of time left, such as preaching, rather than writing books that soon no one would need anyway.

We should not imagine, however, that no writing was being done by Christians. Paul, of course, wrote frequent letters to Christian communities with whom he had worked as a Christian missionary. At least seven of his letters have been preserved in the New Testament. But Paul did not intend to write "Scripture" that Christians would read for centuries when he wrote those letters. He meant for them to substitute for his own presence as he gave advice for problems in those communities. He would have preferred to be with them himself. But since he could not be there, writing a letter was the next best thing. Even then, since it was an oral culture, Paul anticipated that his letters would be read aloud so that the whole community could hear them. Other early Christian missionaries such as Philip or Barnabas may have written similar documents.

As we saw earlier, some pressing, short term needs prompted the composition of brief collections of the stories of Jesus. Christians wrote them to use in worship, or teaching, or missionary preaching, and so on. But, so far as we know, no one before Mark tried to compose a continuous account of the entire career of Jesus.

Circumstances were changing in early Christianity which caused Christians to begin writing down the Jesus traditions in these brief collections. Those same changing circumstances eventually worked to encourage Mark and the other evangelists to compose their Gospels.

The group of apostles and eyewitnesses who had accompanied Jesus during his ministry was diminishing. They were the primary suppliers of the stories about Jesus. They were also the only dependable authorities to correct distortions. If there was uncertainty about a story or even a detail of a story people could ask them "What really happened?" But in just a few years some were already dead and others were getting old. If scholars are correct in dating the composition of the Gospel of Mark in the late sixties then at least two and possibly more of "the Twelve" were dead by then (Peter, James, the son of Zebedee, maybe his brother, John, probably others) as well as the Apostle Paul.

At first most Christians expected Jesus to return quickly. As time went on and he did not return, their anticipation of the Parousia (his second coming) lost its preoccupying vividness. Accordingly the Christian community became much more interested in preserving the Jesus traditions. By recording them they were more readily available as a resource to assist the church. It used them to re-examine its own life in the light of the postponement of Jesus' return.

Collections of Jesus stories also were consolidated and preserved for use in instructing new Christians. As Christian missionaries succeeded in persuading new adherents to the Christian faith, the converts required training in its beliefs and practices. Collections of Jesus traditions served as resources for that educational task. The church also had to begin to reckon with the need to indoctrinate the next generations of Christians.

The worship requirements of early Christian communities had stimulated the writing of some traditions for liturgical use. Early Christians read and reread the same stories during worship, and particularly at major cult rituals and festivals. Christians do something very similar today when they, for example, read and reread the nativity stories during the Christmas season. Or, they return again and again to Paul's account of the institution of the Lord's Supper (1 Cor. 11:23–26) when they observe that worship ritual.

The growth and expansion of Christianity produced differing versions of Christian belief and behavior. Such diversities of religious opinion could lead to serious disagreement and even open conflict. At first the apostles and the elders of the Jerusalem Christian church served as authorities to whom appeal for resolution of arguments could be made. As Christianity spread into new areas the Jerusalem authorities were less accessible. When the size of that group dwindled Christians began to feel the need for some alternate standard for determining acceptable Christian faith and practice.

Some stories of Jesus proved particularly supportive and encouraging to Christians who were persecuted for their belief. As the incidents of persecution increased in number and severity Christians circulated tracts relating stories to sustain those who were suffering. Anecdotes in which Jesus was remembered to have taught about steadfastness in the face of persecution served this purpose. So did Christian recollections of Jesus' submissive obedience to the will of God as he suffered his own martyrdom.

Early Christians were concerned with resolving the problem of their relationship to Judaism. Christianity began as a sect within Judaism. At that stage its appeal to Jewish religious traditions, its use of the Jewish Scriptures, and its adoption of certain Jewish religious customs and practices were understandable. Then the distance between Christianity and Judaism widened and the rift between them became more obvious. Christians were troubled by challenges to their use of elements of the Jewish religion. As the church worked out its self-identity distinct from Judaism, written collections of relevant Jesus traditions were helpful. In some stories Jesus scolded Jewish religious leaders for being hypocritical. In others he urged a deeper and fuller grasp of the real significance of Judaism than his religious Jewish contemporaries had attained. Such stories helped early Christians both to understand and to explain to others the relationship between Christianity and Judaism.

There is yet another reason why the writing down of the stories about Jesus became imperative in early Christianity. As much as early Christians loved those stories which they had heard and told so often, that very love began to corrupt the Jesus traditions. For all of the stories that were handed down about Jesus there were still gaps in his life which those stories did not cover. Further, some of the stories were too short to fully satisfy the eager curiosity of early believers.

The fertile imaginations of popular Christian piety expanded brief accounts, filled in the gaps, even, occasionally, added fictional fabrications to the fund of Jesus traditions.

Abundant examples of these kinds of reverent fictionalizing are available in documents which scholars group together as the New Testament apocrypha. For instance the second century *Epistula Apostolorum* contains extensively expanded accounts of conversations which the risen Jesus had with his apostles. The *Gospel of Peter* explicitly describes the resurrection (G Pet. 35–42). The *Infancy Gospel of Thomas* (end of second century, C.E.), portrays the six-year-old Jesus miraculously carrying water to Mary in his clothes after he tripped and broke the jug (IG Thom. 11:1–2).

As fascinating as those additions to the more ancient stories about Jesus were, early Christians soon became concerned that they not be accorded the same authority as the older apostolic stories. As long as the stories of Jesus were deposited only in the oral traditions it was difficult to distinguish between early recollections and recent accounts. By recording the earliest stories about Jesus in writing, the early church was then able to set them in a class apart from the other popular pious stories. It thereby provided the means for protecting them from distortion and addition.

The factors we have just considered above stimulated early Christians to gather some Jesus traditions into brief collections. The authors of the Synoptic Gospels undoubtedly were affected by many of these same considerations. They drew on those abbreviated collections as sources for their longer documents. They also included other Jesus stories which they obtained from the oral tradition.

In addition to being influenced by the general changes occurring in early Christianity each evangelist had his own special reasons for writing a Gospel. Each author had his own particular theological interests and insights. Each was influenced by the specific needs and troublesome problems which were disturbing his own community. Each was concerned to advance the spiritual well-being of his community by helping to speak to those needs and those problems. It was these burning issues and these theological insights which make each Gospel distinct.

II. THE COMPOSITION OF THE GOSPEL OF MARK

We will consider the Gospel of Mark first because, as we will soon see,[1] scholars consider it to be the earliest of the Synoptic Gospels. They believe Mark was written before either Matthew or Luke.

A. Mark's Literary Characteristics

Mark wrote with a simple, popular literary style. We do not have a list of his sources. (They ordinarily did not add bibliographies to the end of literary works in those days.) We assume that he had access to some brief collections of Jesus traditions. Perhaps he drew from those already in use in his community. Presumably he supplemented those stories with others still being told as independent, self-contained oral anecdotes.

Mark bound the stories of Jesus which he collected from a variety of sources into one continuous, extended narrative. He established the sequence of the stories, often, by the very simple device of using indefinite connectives such as "and," "again," "then," "immediately," "in those days," "then going out," and so on (see Mark 1:9; 2:13; 3:1, 13, 19, 31, etc.). Since the connectives which Mark used were frequently vague and nonspecific his narrative sometimes seems loosely tied together.

Mark supplied additional "narrative glue" (what held his account together) by using narrative anticipation. When a major new development or event was impending Mark provided advance preparation for his hearers. For instance, in Mark 3:9 the disciples are instructed to secure a boat in anticipation of Mark 4:1 when Jesus instructed a large crowd from the boat. Or again, in Mark 11:11 Jesus briefly visited the Temple in Jerusalem in advance of the "cleansing of the Temple" incident (Mark 11:15–19).[2] A third example: Mark described Peter's presence in the courtyard of the high priest (Mark 14:54) in anticipation of the "three-fold denial" anecdote (Mark 14:66–72).

When Mark combined many stories about Jesus into a connected narrative he produced a composite of Jesus. Mark composed his portrait of Jesus with a narrative simplicity marked by a vivid and refreshing sense of realism. Though acknowledging Jesus as Son of

God, Mark is quite candid about his human nature. The moods and emotions which he ascribed to Jesus are richer and more varied than in any of the other canonical Gospels. Jesus becomes angry, tires, hungers, groans, pities, wonders, and so on.

Another feature which is characteristic of Mark's Gospel is his preference for the miracle stories. Compared with the content of the Gospels of Matthew and Luke, Mark recorded a smaller amount of the teachings traditions of Jesus. He stressed those traditions which described Jesus' extraordinary deeds. We will return to this observation when we consider the purposes for which Mark wrote. The prominence of the miraculous in the Gospel of Mark has prompted some scholars to suggest that there may have been an earlier version of Mark. That version, which has not survived, supposedly contained mostly miracle stories. This suggestion of a more primitive version behind the Gospel of Mark in the New Testament has not won wide acceptance.[3]

We can find abundant evidence in the Gospel of Mark that indicates he wrote his Gospel for the benefit of a Gentile Christian community. When he included Aramaic words or alluded to Jewish customs he thoughtfully provided explanations for these foreign elements (Mark 5:41; 7:3–4, 11, 34; 15:22). On the other hand he simply transliterated Latin words into Greek without any clarification (Mark 4:21; 5:9, 15; 12:15; 15:16, 39). Nor did he explain references to Roman coins (Mark 6:37; 12:42; 14:5) or facets of Roman law, even when it contradicted accepted Jewish custom (Mark 10:12). Apparently Mark could count on his community's prior acquaintance with those things.

But even if they were Gentile, how do we know that Mark's intended hearers were Christian? The cumulative effect of several observations seems to leave their Christian identity beyond doubt. Mark used the term "gospel" as a technical term which he assumed his audience knew (Mark 1:1, 14–15; 10:29; 13:10; 14:9). He introduced unidentified characters into his narrative (so, John the Baptist in Mark 1:4; Simon and Andrew in 1:16, and frequently elsewhere), expecting his readers to recognize them on their own. In addition, he assumed throughout his entire work that his readers already knew the stories and teachings of Jesus.

B. Mark's Literary Accomplishment

During the early stages of form criticism (which we discussed in the first chapter) some scholars badly undervalued Mark's literary achievement. They simplistically described him as being little more than a collector of the oral traditions about Jesus. His contribution as editor was thought of as mainly that of stringing the beads of the oral tradition into a narrative necklace. Scholars now generally recognize that view to be a serious underestimation of the literary ingenuity and theological investment which Mark brought to his task. As is true with each one of the Gospels, the Gospel of Mark must be granted its own autonomy as a theologically informed and motivated religious work. Our acknowledgement and appreciation of the integrity of the composition for its own sake is essential for our interpretive understanding. We misuse the Gospels if we regard them simply as colorless source documents from which we may draw information to construct a composite reproduction of the "real" Jesus. Each Gospel is a distinct, theologically formed portrait of the same Lord of the church of the Easter faith.

Mark's recording of the earlier oral tradition material was not motivated solely by antiquarian interest. He did not record the stories of Jesus in an extended narrative form just to preserve old folk tales. When he wrote those traditions down he wanted to update, adapt, and apply them to the needs of his community. This observation has both negative and positive implications.

Negatively, Mark did not write his Gospel to "do history." That does not mean he was not interested in Jesus as a historical person. It does suggest that he wrote the Gospel for purposes other than simply passing on informational data.

On the basis of the nature of the pre-Markan forms of the Jesus traditions which we discussed in Chapter One it follows that the order of events in the Markan narrative is not a very reliable guide for the chronological reconstruction of Jesus' public ministry except in the broadest, most general terms. Though a few segments of the sequence may have been established in some of the brief pre-Markan collections, the order of the narrative is mainly the product of Mark's own redaction.

With this recognition we discover important clues to Mark's special theological interests. It is in the ordering of the units of the tradition and in the editorial connectives which Mark provided to join them into narrative sequence that we discern most clearly his special theological emphases. So, for example, geographical references and "messianic secret" motifs, (both features will be discussed later), occur mainly in the connective links. The cumulative interpretive effect which the ordering of accounts together can have may be observed in Mark 2:1—3:6. Mark accumulated individual conflict traditions into an extended series of controversies, one following the other. This produced the effect of intensifying the hostility which Jesus' enemies directed toward him. Mark explicitly confirmed his purpose in this section with the concluding verse: Jesus' enemies plot to destroy him (Mark 3:6).

Positively, Mark's major literary achievement was that of taking the various types of Jesus traditions and welding them to the church's preaching of the crucified and risen Christ. He thereby established controls and set limits for the interpretation of the traditions. He also firmly anchored the church's cross-event proclamation in the history of the earthly Jesus. He was employing the Jesus traditions to provide a broad narrational history which embodied a saving event of eternal dimensions. He described that saving event in the climax to his work, the Passion narrative.

We are thereby forced to regard all of the episodes in the public ministry of Jesus as anticipatory prefigurements of the passion. That is, each incident is obscure (and even misleading and deceptive) until it is interpreted from the controlling perspective of the crucifixion and resurrection. We cannot fully understand what Jesus' call of the first disciples meant (Mark 1:16–20), or his feeding of the five thousand (Mark 6:30–44), or his being anointed with expensive oil (Mark 14:3–9) until we hear these stories in the light of Good Friday and Easter. This was what led a German scholar to describe Mark as "passion narrative with an extended introduction."[4]

C. The Literary Unity of Mark

Mark composed his Gospel as a single literary work. It was not a collection of stories about Jesus. It was the story of Jesus, the Son of God. Mark intended that it be read in its entirety. When we fail to do so we miss perceiving important features of his story which he developed over extended sections of the narrative. Yet regularly in contemporary worship services Christians read and hear expounded only individual sections from Mark's Gospel. When that occurs they are really being confronted by forms of Jesus stories from the pre-Markan tradition (though they have perhaps been modified by Mark). But they are not hearing the Gospel of Mark.

For example, only when we read the Gospel of Mark straight through, as a single story, do we notice the development of the major groups of characters, the "actors," in the Markan narrative drama. Unless we read the Gospel in its entirety we miss the movement of roles Mark assigned to the religious leaders, the crowds, most important of all, the disciples.

The Jewish religious leaders (Pharisees, scribes, priests, etc.) are the enemies of Jesus throughout. Mark took care to picture them as those whose hostility intensifies from hypercritical resentment (Mark 2:6–7) to murderous antipathy (Mark 11:18; 14:1–2) and who, finally, are responsible for his unjust execution.[5]

The crowds of people provide sharp contrast to the animosity of the religious leaders (Mark juxtaposes both reactions numerous times: Mark 2:6–12; 3:1–12; 3:20–22; etc.). They embody popular unreflective enthusiasm, and flock to Jesus, eager for his teaching and captivated by his miracles. The few instances when they respond negatively (5:17; 6:2–6) anticipate the time when their fickle allegiance shifts to the enemies of Jesus, the religious leaders (14:43; 15:8, 11). The disciples, especially the Twelve, are that part of the crowd who enter into a closer relationship with Jesus. Their initial imperceptiveness about who he really is, and what his work is really about deteriorates into purposeful, intentional misunderstanding that culminates in abandonment. They are "obtuse, obdurate, recalcitrant men who at first are unperceptive of Jesus' messiahship, then oppose its style and character, and finally totally reject it."[6]

III. MARK'S PURPOSES

As we have seen Mark must have had compelling reasons which moved him to compose his Gospel. He did not write it simply as a hobby to entertain himself in his idle moments. Neither was he solely interested in gathering together as many facts as possible about the earthly career of Jesus so others who read his work would know more about him. Mark wrote to be of service to his own community.

A. Increase Faith

Mark's primary purpose in writing his Gospel was to strengthen his community's faith in Jesus as the Christ, the resurrected Son of God. He composed his connected story of Jesus out of well-known independent stories about Jesus to evoke a more intense commitment. We should therefore think of the Gospel of Mark in its entirety as one proclamation. It is not a collection of anecdotes about Jesus. It is a unified presentation of Mark's own faith, whose reading, Mark fervently hoped, would call forth strong belief from the reader. As Willi Marxsen has described it, "The evangelist proclaims the One who once appeared as the One who is to come, and who . . . is present now as the proclamation is made."[7]

It is interesting to note that Mark's very act of writing the story of Jesus tended to work against this primary goal. When early Christians told stories of Jesus to illustrate their gospel preaching, those stories shared in the atmosphere of the urgency to respond which that preaching created. Mark collected the stories and used them as parts of his one written story of Jesus. In so doing he removed from them that atmosphere of urgency. He historicized those stories. That is, potentially, salvation was being presented as something belonging to the past.[8] One of Mark's major editorial tasks was to counteract that effect. He did so by presenting Jesus in the narrative as the savior who presents God's claim on the reader (or hearer) in the act of reading the work itself.

B. Important Theological Ideas

1. Mark's Doctrine of Christ

Mark's understanding of who Jesus was is reflected in the titles which he used to refer to Jesus in his Gospel. The titles which appear most frequently are "Rabbi," "Christ," "Son of man," "Son of God."

In spite of the fact that the title "Rabbi" or "Teacher" occurs often, these titles did not carry great theological meaning for Mark. The titles were terms of respect used to address learned persons (in the case of "Rabbi," great teachers of the Jewish law). They did not necessarily indicate any unique, messianic concept. The terms probably appeared frequently as forms of respectful address in the oral stories about Jesus' teachings. Although Mark had great respect for the teaching traditions he preferred to emphasize those stories which described Jesus' miraculous deeds. We'll see why later.

The title, "Christ," is, of course, derived from the Greek translation of the Hebrew "Messiah." A curious thing occurs in Mark with regard to this title. Mark included three traditions in which Jesus was described as speaking the title (Mark 9:41; 12:35; 13:21). But in none of them does he explicitly apply it to himself. Twice when others applied the title to him in his hearing (Mark 8:29; 14:61) Jesus responded with a saying referring to the "Son of man" (see below) which appears to be offered as a corrective to the use of the title "Christ." And this in spite of the fact that Mark considered the title to be perfectly appropriate when applied to Jesus (Mark 1:1). Mark even seemed to be used to others calling him and his fellow Christians by that name (Mark 9:41). This strongly suggests that though Mark believed that Jesus was the Messiah promised in the Jewish Scriptures, he used the messianic title "Christ" guardedly because it was being misunderstood by some in his community.

The title "Son of man" plays a prominent role in the Gospel of Mark. The title had its roots in the Jewish religious traditions, though scholars are uncertain about the precise stages in its pre-Christian development. Its Jewish heritage made it readily expressive of a more than human figure who will come in power and glory at the end of the world. Mark was familiar with that significance (Mark 8:38; 13:26; 14:62). But he balanced that meaning of "Son of man" with another which was very important for him. He used it prominently in the middle section of his Gospel (see the section on Mark's structure later in this chapter) where he was concerned with the identity of Jesus. Three times Jesus used Son of man sayings not to portray end-time glory but to predict his fate (Mark 8:31; 9:31; 10:33–34). The Son of man must be rejected, delivered up, must suffer, be killed, and rise again. In Mark's use of "Son of man" the themes of glory and authority converge with the necessity for suffering. Mark wanted it understood that no view of Christ is complete unless both dimensions are present.

Another title for Jesus which Mark emphasized was "Son of God." That it was particularly meaningful for Mark is indicated by his use of it both at the beginning (Mark 1:1) and at the end (15:39) of his Gospel. Again we find the roots for the title firmly embedded in Jewish religious traditions as reflected in the Jewish Scriptures. For Mark the title expressed Jesus' unique relationship to God. The identity of Jesus as Son of God was incontestable. The demons whom Jesus cast out recognized him (Mark 3:11). God himself acclaimed Jesus as his Son at his baptism (Mark 1:11) and again at the transfiguration (Mark 9:7). Even a non-believer who was present at the crucifixion perceived Jesus' true identity (15:39). The purpose of Mark's Gospel is to argue how much more those confronted with the good news of the resurrection (i.e., Mark's own community) ought to acknowledge Jesus as Son of God—just as Mark does himself (Mark 1:1).

2. Jesus, the Agent of God

As we saw earlier Mark placed great emphasis on the miracle stories. He stressed the miracle traditions to present Jesus as the special agent of God. Behind this aspect of Mark's "Jesus portrait" was the belief common to early Christians (and others) that God and Satan were locked in a massive cosmic struggle.[9] Satan had usurped God's right to rule in his creation. God willed to win it back.

Mark portrayed Jesus as the special agent of God. He was endowed with supernatural power and authority. His mission was to inaugurate God's reclamation of his creation. Through Jesus God was restoring his right to rule over the whole of his created order.

When Jesus calmed the storm (Mark 6:47–52), he was replacing the chaos characteristic of Satan's rule with that order which God had once established over the chaotically stormy waters at creation. When Jesus healed or restored to life (Mark 5:21–43) he was restoring life-force where there was death or its potential, on behalf of God who created life. When Jesus cast out demons (Mark 1:23–28) he was routing agents of Satan in order that God might once again rule in human hearts. Though Satan did his worst through those over whom he ruled by causing them to kill Jesus, God vindicated him as his agent by raising him from the dead. In Jesus' deeds and in his ultimate fate God showed himself to be the life-giver. He won the cosmic struggle with Satan and his forces of Death.

3. Persecution and the End of the World

Mark's community was living in turbulent times and Mark wanted them to understand the turmoil theologically. The political unrest stirred by the insurrection of Jewish nationalists against Rome was increasing in intensity. Recently a savage persecution of Christians in Rome had been ordered by the Emperor Nero (Tacitus *Annals* XV:44). News of the martyrdoms of both Peter and Paul was probably fresh in their minds. Now Mark's own community was facing the prospect of persecution. They may have already suffered its initial onslaughts.

Apparently the community was encountering opposition from two fronts. People were not responding with faith to their preaching. Mark argues repeatedly that unbelief and hardness of heart in response to their preaching was extremely serious and would be recompensed. This was especially true of the leaders of a Judaism which had rejected the gospel and had become more intense in its enmity toward Christianity. Mark's community was also facing (and perhaps already experiencing) persecution from pagan authorities, and Mark was eager to strengthen them in their resolve to stand fast against such suffering.

Mark related the realities of his community's situation to their belief that Jesus would return soon and the world would end. Unrest and wars and persecutions were signs of the impending end (Mark 13:7–9). Mark's community was living in a time impregnated with the quality of end-time urgency (Mark 4:29; 9:1; 12:1–11). But Mark did not want them to go overboard with end-of-the-world fanaticism. Though the time was near, the end had not actually already begun (Mark 13:6–7, 10, 21–23). No one should allow extreme expectations to disillusion and disappoint them when Jesus' second coming was delayed yet a little while. There was still an interim time before Jesus' return when Christians must remain faithful and alert.

This belief in the nearness of the end of the world provided Mark with the perspective to help his community cope with the sufferings which threatened them. Persecution was one sign of the approach of Jesus' second coming. Christians were to undergo suffering and distress as a prelude to his return. As Jesus had fulfilled his mission through suffering so were they to be supported and strengthened by his example. The first disciples had faced the same perils and hatred which Jesus had known. So must the Christians of Mark's community conduct themselves (Mark 13:9–13). Suffering Son of man set the model for suffering discipleship (Mark 8:31, 34–38; 10:33–34, 38–40). Perhaps Mark emphasized the denial of Peter (Mark 14:29–31, 53–72) to encourage some in his own community who had already denied their faith during persecution.

In all of this Mark was not simply hoping that his fellow-Christians would become more accurately informed about what Jesus did before he was killed, or where he did it, or to whom. "Mark was concerned to teach that the theological meaning of the cross can best be understood by one who has humbly prepared himself for a renunciation of self, for a life of service and, if need be, of suffering and martyrdom."[10]

IV. SPECIAL FEATURES OF MARK'S GOSPEL

A. Structure

Mark carefully structured his narrative to throw some of the issues and the needs confronting his community into sharper focus. The Gospel divides into two almost equal parts. The literary "hinge" joining the two parts is Peter's confession of Jesus as "Christ" (Mark 8:27–30).

The first half describes Jesus' ministry in Galilee. Galilee was more than a geographical designation; Mark invested it with theological meaning.[11] It stood for the disclosure of Jesus as the end-time agent of God. It also represented the inauguration of the mission to the Gentiles (see especially the exorcism of the Syrophoenician's daughter, Mark 7:25-30). It was this stage in the expansion of Christianity which extended to include Mark's own community. Throughout the first half of his Gospel, Mark placed primary emphasis upon the powerful deeds of Jesus. He confronted both the hostile civil and religious leaders and the demons with the invincible authority of the hidden Messiah. He taught and preached with an authority far surpassing theirs, and he miraculously subdued the supernatural forces opposed to God.

The disciples, who had been chosen by him and who had responded to his call, were intimately associated with Jesus throughout this period of his ministry. Mark portrayed them as attracted to Jesus and fascinated by his deeds. But they were unable to comprehend the real meaning of it all. They simply could not believe who he was disclosed to be or what he was about.

The second half of Mark's Gospel turns toward Jerusalem which Mark interpreted negatively. It stood for the opposition, hostility, and rejection which culminated in Jesus' execution. It symbolized that unresponsiveness and hardheartedness which result in unbelief.

Whereas the characteristic emphasis of the first half was on the miracles of Jesus, the second half emphasized his Passion and its implications for discipleship. Three times he predicted his suffering death and immediately followed it with instructions about the suffering servant nature of authentic discipleship (Mark 8:31-38; 9:31-37; 10:32-45). The disciples intentionally misunderstood both his words about himself and his instructions concerning discipleship. They would not accept what he disclosed to them. Consequently with the climax to the narrative, the Passion, they all failed him (Mark 14: 18-21, 37-50, 66-72).

The confession which Peter made of Jesus as "the Christ" (Mark 8:27-30) is the fulcrum upon which Mark balanced the two halves of his narrative. At the point at which the confession occurs in the narrative account Peter accurately identified who Jesus was, but for the wrong reasons. Jesus' activity up until then was primarily that of doing miraculous deeds and teaching marvelous wisdom. If that was all the disciples knew about Jesus they were not yet able to say who he was. Neither Peter nor any of the others knew enough about Jesus yet to understand fully what kind of "Christ" (Messiah) he was. That was possible only when they gave full consideration to the cross. So Jesus "corrected" Peter's understanding of his messiahship by speaking of the need of the Son of man to suffer (Mark 8:31). (Mark included two more suffering "Son of man" predictions by Jesus [Mark 9:31; 10:32–34], so the point would not be missed). When Peter refused that concept of "Christ" Jesus harshly rebuked him (Mark 8:32–33). If that was not what Peter meant by "Christ" then he did not know Jesus as "Christ." It was later in the courtyard (Mark 14:66–72) when Jesus' messianic identity as suffering Son of man had become evident that Peter's confession would have counted for something, but then he denied instead.[12]

B. Confusion with "Divine Man"

We may be touching here on another, secondary goal which Mark had in writing his Gospel. It is possible that one of the compelling causes which encouraged him to compose his narrative story of Jesus was a failure Christians from his community were experiencing in their gospel preaching. The stories of Jesus, told as isolated independent anecdotes, were not clarifying and illustrating as successfully as they once had. Those stories did not encourage belief in Jesus as the crucified and resurrected Son of God, the Christ. Instead Christians were frustrated to find that the Jesus stories they told confused their hearers rather than clarified. How could that be?

A figure that was popular in the pagan Hellenistic culture was the "divine man." Divine men were people who claimed to have access to supernatural power. They demonstrated their capabilities by doing magical tricks, conjuring up supernatural spirits, miraculously healing people, exorcising demons, and doing other similar activities.

The average person in the first century experienced the world as a hostile place. Things were continually happening which affected one's health, family, prosperity, and business interests. Yet one rarely had control over those influences which were affecting him or her. People often regarded all such influences as the effect which supernatural beings were having upon their lives.

Chronic, acute indigestion, for example, was the result of a curse some rival had had brought upon them, or was caused by a supernatural spirit, a demon, which possessed them. They did not know about the "plop-plop, fizz-fizz" fast relief that a glass of seltzer could bring. Instead they superstitiously turned for aid to a "divine man" who claimed access to supernatural powers and was believed to have control over supernatural beings. They also looked to such persons for advice and counsel, predictions for the future, protection for important undertakings, aid against competitors and rivals, and so on.

This popular Hellenistic superstition raised difficulties for Christian gospel preaching which had not been present when Jews were the primary audience. These Gentile people did not know much about the Messiah (Christ) figure of the Jewish religious traditions. Christians told them stories of Jesus' calming the storm, or healing the paralytic, or giving advice about divorce, or exorcising a demon. To the Gentile non-Christian those stories sounded like the familiar exploits of another "divine man." "Christ" must be like the Hellenistic wonder worker.

Those non-believing Gentiles were filling the word "Christ" as a title for Jesus with much the same content that Mark pictured Peter doing with his confession at Caesarea Philippi. The title was right but its meaning was incomplete. They must, along with Peter, acknowledge that other part of Jesus' mission as the Christ. They must include his suffering crucifixion and being raised by God in their confession of him as "Christ." Then he was clearly set apart from all "divine men." He was the unique Son of God.

It was not that the stories about Jesus had changed. People just heard them differently. Mark was helping his community adjust its preaching to its audience.

C. "Messianic Secret"

A famous feature of the Markan narrative which we have only alluded to until now is the "messianic secret" motif. This motif runs through most of Mark's Gospel.[13] Scholars have pointed out a number of traits in the Gospel of Mark through which the recognition of the messianic identity of Jesus as the Christ, the Son of God actually seems to be suppressed.

For instance, Jesus repeatedly imposed commands to silence on demons and unclean spirits which he exorcised (Mark 1:23–25, 34; 3:11–12). Mark described Jesus as forbidding people whom he had healed from telling others about their good fortune (Mark 1:43–44; 5:43; 7:36). He even prohibited his disciples from telling others about him (Mark 8:30; 9:9). He tried to conceal his presence from others (Mark 7:24; 9:30). Some scholars also point to the private teachings, which Jesus limited to his disciples (Mark 4:33–34; 7:17–23; 13:3–37).

These features almost always occur in the redactional material, the narrative connectors with which Mark bound his story together. That would suggest that most of them were not included in the independent stories of the oral tradition. Mark himself was the one largely responsible for the prominence which the "messianic secret" motif had in his Gospel. Further, the secrecy theme abruptly disappeared when Jesus stood as the accused on trial before the high priest (14:61–62). Why? What was Mark indicating with his emphasis on secrecy about Jesus' identity as Messiah (Christ) before his passion?

The "messianic secret" feature helped Mark deal further with the problem which members of his community were having when they tried to use the stories of Jesus. It was an additional antidote for the potential danger that Gentiles might misunderstand those stories as picturing Jesus as a Hellenistic "divine man."

Through the secrecy motif Mark insisted that the identity of Jesus was not solved with just one story. A healing did not define the richness of his messiahship. Neither did an exorcism. Not even a heavenly epiphany (a manifestation of the presence of God) such as the transfiguration (Mark 9:2–10) was enough. Only when the portrait of Jesus was completed by including his suffering and crucifixion was he seen to be both Christ of glory and power and suffering Son of man.

The stories about Jesus are partial by themselves. Only when they are heard and interpreted in terms of the cross event do they correctly show his messiahship. Mark was restoring the functional usability of those stories to clarify the gospel preaching.

D. The Ending of the Gospel

As we can observe in most modern editions of the New Testament the ending of Mark's Gospel has been somewhat problematic. The most ancient Greek manuscripts of Mark conclude with 16:8. Scholars, with few exceptions, regard the various alternative extensions which other manuscripts contain as later additions appended by unknown Christians to provide a more satisfactory conclusion. The divergence in the vocabulary and literary style of those last few added verses compared with the literary style in the rest of the Gospel confirms the manuscript evidence.

There is no consensus among scholars, however, concerning whether Mark really ended his Gospel with 16:8. Some scholars think the original conclusion was lost quite early as the result of manuscript mutilation. That was a frequent occurrence with the beginning and ending of brittle papyrus scrolls. After scrolls had been unrolled and rolled back up again repeatedly the ends of the scrolls, which suffered the most wear, often broke off. Certainly the present ending is very abrupt and grammatically awkward. In addition, Mark 14:28 and 16:7 seem to anticipate appearances of Jesus, the accounts of which could well have been included in a "lost" ending.

On the other hand, the problem with our explaining Mark's abrupt conclusion by assuming mutilation is not only that it is only a theory but that such loss would have had to occur quite early. Neither Matthew nor Luke, who both used copies of Mark, knew any of the extant longer endings. The lack of appearance accounts is an argument which assumes the unprovable existence of post-resurrection appearance traditions prior to Mark's composition.

Although the ending at 16:8 is grammatically awkward it is not unique. Mark has equally rough grammatical constructions elsewhere. The final description of the women's fearful flight is very appropriate for a community caught in the grips of panic as it was facing persecution. Such a conclusion forces the question, "What is *your* response to the Easter proclamation?" It seems best, then, for us to regard 16:8 as the original conclusion.

V. WHO WAS MARK?

As much as we would like to answer the question of the identity of the author of the second Gospel with absolute certainty we must recall what we said at the end of the first chapter. All of the Gospels in the New Testament are anonymous works.[14] Their authors did not explicitly identify themselves for our benefit.

Nevertheless the association of the name "Mark" with the second Gospel was quite ancient. The earliest mention of the name occurs in an early church historian (Eusebius—early fourth century) who quoted an earlier bishop (Papias—middle second century). That tradition described Mark as the interpreter of Peter, who had not known Jesus himself, but wrote down the stories of Jesus which Peter told. Unfortunately there is nothing in the second Gospel which confirms that description.

"Mark" (Marcus) was a very common name in the first century Greco-Roman world. Most people have assumed that "Mark" was the Mark mentioned frequently in other New Testament literature (Acts 12:12, 25; 13:13; Col. 4:10; 2 Tim. 4:11; Philem. 24). Again we are at a loss to point to evidence in the Gospel itself which supports this identification.

From time to time someone will suggest that the author left us a clue to his identity with the reference to the young man who fled naked from the garden (Mark 14:51–52), but that is unlikely. If it is a clue it is so oblique that we can make nothing of it.

About the best we can do is to describe the author as an unknown first century Gentile Christian.

Similar uncertainties surround the problem of provenance. The Gospel does not explicitly indicate its place of origin nor may it be conclusively inferred. Suggestions have included Rome, Syrian Antioch, Galilee, Alexandria. All are possible, none are necessary. The date of composition fares hardly better. Since Mark 13:5–7, 14 seem to indicate some knowledge of events which led up to the Jewish war against Rome (66–70 C.E.), and Mark 13:14–20 assumes that the Temple was not yet destroyed (70 C.E.), most scholars date the writing of the Gospel in the late 60s. Nevertheless even here the data are inconclusive.[15]

VI. OUTLINE OF THE GOSPEL OF MARK

I. Introduction 1:1–13
  A. The message of John the Baptist 1:1–8
  B. Baptism of Jesus 1:9–11
  C. Temptation 1:12–13

II. The ministry of Jesus in and around Galilee 1:14—8:26
  A. In Galilee 1:14—5:43
     1. Ministry of teaching and miracles 1:14–45
        a. The preaching of Jesus 1:14–15
        b. Call of the first disciples 1:16–20
        c. Summary: teaching with authority 1:21–22
        d. Exorcism and healings 1:23–38
        e. Summary: preaching and teaching 1:39
        f. Healing of leper 1:40–45
     2. Conflicts and controversies 2:1—3:35
        a. Healing of the paralytic 2:1–12
        b. Call of Levi 2:13–14
        c. Criticism of table-fellowship 2:15–17
        d. Question of fasting 2:18–22
        e. Controversies over sabbath observance 2:23—3:6
        f. Withdrawal and appointment of the Twelve 3:7–19
        g. Controversies over the source of Jesus' power 3:20–30
        h. True relatives of Jesus 3:31–35
     3. Teaching by the sea 4:1–34
        a. Parable of the soils 4:1–9
        b. Theory of parable confusion 4:1–12
        c. Allegorical interpretation 4:13–20
        d. Parables of the kingdom 4:21–32
        e. Summary: a private explanation of parables 4:33–34
     4. Miracles by the sea 4:35—5:43
        a. Subduing the storm 4:35–41
        b. The Gerasene demoniac 5:1–20
        c. Jairus' daughter ill 5:21–24
        d. Healing of woman with hemorrhage 5:25–34
        e. Resuscitation of Jairus' daughter 5:35–43
  B. Around the Galilean region 6:1—8:26
     1. Opposition stimulates expansion of mission 6:1–29
        a. Rejection in Nazareth 6:1–6
        b. The Twelve sent out 6:7–13
        c. John the Baptist killed by Herod 6:14–29
     2. Clear signs for those who hear and see 6:30—8:26

      c. Tribute to Caesar 12:13–17
      d. Controversy about resurrection 12:18–27
      e. The greatest commandment 12:28–34
      f. David foretold the Messiah 12:35–37
      g. Warning against the scribes 12:38–40
      h. The widow's mite 12:41–44
3. End-time discourse 13:1–37
      a. Impending destruction of the Temple 13:1–2
      b. Signs preceding the end 13:3–13
      c. Signs heralding the end 13:14–31
      d. Time of the end's coming uncertain 13:32–37
4. Anticipation of passion 14:1–42
      a. The resolve to kill Jesus 14:1–2
      b. Anointing in Bethany 14:3–9
      c. Judas resolves to betray Jesus 14:10–11
      d. Last Passover meal 14:12–25
      e. Anticipation of disciples' abandonment 14:26–31
      f. Gethsemane 14:32–42
5. Cross event 14:43—16:8
      a. Betrayal and arrest 14:43–52
      b. Jesus condemned by the high council 14:53–65
      c. Denial by Peter 14:66–72
      d. Trial before Pilate 15:1–15
      e. The humiliation 15:16–20
      f. Crucifixion 15:21–41
      g. The burial 15:42–47
      h. The women at the empty tomb 16:1–8

The major divisions in this outline reflect observations which were made previously concerning the literary structure of the Markan narrative.[16]

VII. INTERRELATIONSHIP OF THE FIRST THREE GOSPELS

So far we have given specific attention only to the Gospel of Mark. When we broaden our perspective to include all of the first three Gospels the complexities which we have encountered in trying to understand the nature of Mark's Gospel are compounded. A comparative reading of the first three Gospels reveals both striking similarities and sharp differences.

A. Literary Dependency

Students of the Bible have been aware of the extensive similarities in the Synoptic Gospels for a long time. Throughout the centuries of the church's life most Christians explained this phenomenon in what was for them the only conceivable way. The first three Gospels were similar because, in the providence of God, they had roots which extended back independently to a common apostolic witness. A few early scholars such as Augustine (who died in 430 C.E.) thought that the Gospels might be interdependent. But most Christians accounted for their similarities by assuming they all drew on the same information. Vestiges of that ancient explanation still appear occasionally in, for example, suggestions of an ancient lost (oral?) apostolic Gospel which served as the source for the independent composition of the canonical Gospels.

Most scholars today support a different solution to the question of similarities between the Gospels. They are convinced that there is a direct literary dependency between the first three Gospels. On the basis of that conviction they struggle with the challenge to describe the complicated literary interrelationship of the Synoptic Gospels in such a way as to account for both the differences and the similarities. That challenge has come to be called "the synoptic problem." In the history of modern biblical scholarship it was first posed in the latter part of the eighteenth century.

The criteria which scholars of literature have defined as supporting some assumption of literary dependency include:

1) telling the same story (common subject matter)
2) telling the story in the same order (correspondence of sequence and continuity of events)
3) telling the story in the same way (similar sentence and word order)
4) telling the story with the same words (extensive vocabulary agreement, use of the same harsh grammatical constructions or unusual words)

When these criteria are applied to the Gospels they produce persuasive results. It is obvious that the first three Gospels tell the same story. The statistics for the common subject matter indicate that of the 661 verses in Mark's narrative ninety percent are in the Gospel of Matthew (some 606 verses which Matthew compressed into about 500 verses in his narrative) and fifty percent are in the Gospel of Luke (over 300 verses).[17]

Telling the story in the same order is confirmed when we notice that the Markan narrative outline is almost entirely reproduced by the other two Synoptic Gospels. Luke conforms more closely to the early part of Mark's sequence and Matthew to the later. With regard to similar sentence and word order we have simply to consult a harmony of the Gospels (the canonical Gospels printed in parallel columns)[18] to discover quickly instance after instance of remarkable likeness in that regard (cf. Mark 1:40–45 and parallels, or Mark 2:1–12 and parallels, and frequently elsewhere).

Probably the most significant criterion for indicating literary dependency is the measure of the rate of vocabulary agreement. In those sections of Matthew which relate the same traditions as in Mark the incidence of the use of the same words is over seventy-three percent. Luke used about sixty-six percent of Mark's words (the correspondence escalates to sixty-nine percent with words of Jesus material common to Luke and Mark).[19] If we look at the end-time discourse of Jesus we find large blocks of material which are word for word the same (Mark 13:5–8, 14–17, 28–32 and parallels).[20]

A famous example of the exact reproduction of an unusual grammatical construction is found in the tradition of the healing of the paralytic (Mark 2:1–12 and parallels). Jesus abruptly interrupted his remarks to the critical scribes without finishing the sentence he had begun, and addressed the paralytic directly. That is a feature which is present in all three versions (Matt. 9:6; Mark 2:10; Luke 5:24). Furthermore, it is the kind of awkward construction that usually did not long survive the abrasive polishing effect that the process of oral transmission had on harsh or unusual grammatical expressions.

B. Priority of Mark

Although we may have given the impression above that Mark was the first of the three evangelists to compose his Gospel the evidence just listed does not necessarily establish that. All that we can conclude by those criteria is that the probability of literary dependency between the first three Gospels is high, and that Mark's Gospel is the common term between the Gospel of Matthew and the Gospel of Luke. We could explain the data by the theory that Matthew was written first, then Mark condensed Matthew, and Luke used both. Theoretically, it also could be argued that Luke wrote first, was used as a source by Mark and then Matthew consulted both in composing his Gospel.

The view that Mark was written first and then was employed as a source by both Matthew and Luke developed from suggestions first formulated by German New Testament scholars in the nineteenth century (Karl Lachmann—1835, H. J. Holtzmann—1863, Bernhard Weiss—1886). Although most scholars today assume the priority of Mark, the thesis of Matthean priority (Augustine's solution) is occasionally proposed, and lately with observable impact.[21]

G. M. Styler has convincingly argued[22] that the decisive consideration in favor of Markan priority and against the priority of Matthew are those passages in Matthew's Gospel which show changes that indicate the Markan version has been misunderstood. We may observe this phenomenon by comparing the two versions of the death of John the Baptist (Matt. 14:3–12; Mark 6:17–29). According to Mark, Herod esteemed John and listened gladly to him, but stood in awe of him. Herodias was the one who wanted to kill him and deviously succeeded. Matthew's abbreviated version described Herod himself as wanting to kill John. That is at odds with Matthew's introduction to the story and contradicts the observation he retained that Herod was sorry to kill him. In addition the context for the two accounts indicates that Matthew missed the development of the narrative flow which Mark sustained (compare Matt. 14:12–13 with 14:1–2).[23]

A number of other considerations support the presumption of the priority of Mark. The argument for Matthean priority fails for want of an explanation of the omissions Mark would thereby have had to make intentionally. There is no clear reason to account for why Mark would have chosen to include some of the material from his source Gospel (Matthew) and left out other equally important sections. We saw above that the same arrangement of the narrative content is visible in all three Gospels. In support of Markan priority we may note that Matthew and Luke follow the same order of events in telling the story of Jesus so long as their common order is paralleled in Mark. When they departed from Mark's order, however, they also diverged from each other. Nowhere do Matthew and Luke diverge in common against Mark's order, although both have additional material which precedes and extends beyond the scope of Mark's account.

With regard to verbal agreement both Matthew and Luke agree more with Mark in parallel sections than they do with each other (Luke with Matthew—only forty-two percent; Luke with Mark—sixty-six percent; Matthew with Mark—seventy-three percent). Matthew and Luke rarely agree in diverging from Mark's wording (Matthew and Luke against Mark—a little over five percent). Most of those few instances are obvious stylistic corrections.

Matthew and Luke frequently improved Mark's grammar and style (151 historical present tenses in Mark were reduced to 21 in Matthew and 1 in Luke). They eliminated unnecessary repetition in Mark (Mark 1:32 and parallels; 2:25 and parallels). They removed picturesque but unessential detail from the Markan version (e.g., the cushion on which Jesus was sleeping, Mark 4:38 and parallels; cf. Mark 5:3–5 and parallels; 5:26–27 and parallels; and often elsewhere). They corrected errors in Mark's account (Mark 1:2–3 and parallels —the Malachi text was removed from the conflated prophetic citation in Mark to make the quotation conform to the introductory formula referring only to Isaiah; Matthew corrected Mark's "Eloi" to "Eli" —Mark 15:34 and parallel).

Both later evangelists often modified or excised features of the Markan narrative which they found offensive. They refined Mark's portrait of Jesus (eliminated references to Jesus' human emotions: Mark 3:5 and parallels; Mark 10:14 and parallels; adjusted Jesus' identity: Mark 6:3 and parallel; modified hints of inability: Mark 6:5 and parallel; cf. also Mark 4:38 and parallels; Mark 10:17–18 and parallels). They also rehabilitated the disciples from what they felt was Mark's unfavorable presentation (cf. Mark 4:13 and parallels; Mark 6:51–52 and parallel; Mark 8:17–18 and parallel; Mark 10:35 and parallel).

On the probability of the priority of Mark it would not be inappropriate for us to think of Matthew and Luke as two different revised, corrected, and expanded second editions of the Gospel of Mark. Their extensive use of Mark as a source for their own compositions testifies to the extremely high regard in which they and their communities held Mark.

VIII. THE "Q" SOURCE

A. Material Common Only to Matthew and Luke

Once our attention turns from the traditions Matthew and Luke have in common with Mark to those pericopes (self-contained units of tradition) they included in their Gospels in addition to Mark's material, we make another interesting discovery. The same criteria which stimulated scholars to formulate a theory of literary dependency between all three Gospels[24] apply equally to the material which Matthew and Luke have in common but which is not present in Mark.

There are between 200 and 250 verses of common traditions in Matthew and Luke which display a combination of similarities and differences with each other similar to those they had in common with Mark. That would suggest the possibility that they were both drawing from another written source or sources besides Mark for this material.

When we apply the criteria for establishing literary dependency we find that the content is similar (compare the temptation of Jesus —Luke 4:1-13 and the parallel in Matthew; the cure of the centurion's slave—Luke 7:1-10 and parallel, etc.). A common general outline is also discernible to a degree. If we remove and isolate the material common to Matthew and Luke, Luke's ordering of that material coincides with Matthew's (with two minor exceptions) through Luke 11:32. From Luke 12 on the material which Matthew has in common with Luke is interspersed throughout his Gospel in no discernible order.

We can easily recognize the correspondence of sentence and word order (compare Luke 7:24-35 and parallel; Luke 12:2-9 and parallel). The rate of vocabulary identity varies widely from very high (of the 72 Greek words in the description of the preaching of John the Baptist, Luke 3:7-9 and parallel, 69 are identical) to only rather approximate (compare the Lord's Prayer tradition, Luke 11:2-4 and parallel). Very few rough grammatical constructions and unusual words occur which should not surprise us. The way in which both evangelists "corrected" Mark rather frequently in these matters would lead us to suspect that they would exercise the same jurisdiction over other source material they incorporated. Nevertheless there are a few, such as the rare Greek word for "daily bread" in the Lord's Prayer (Luke 11:3 and parallel).

The cumulative effect of such data has led scholars to suggest that some theory of literary dependency is the best explanation of the evidence. Direct dependence of Matthew on Luke or the reverse seems excluded. We have already seen that their common possession of Markan material cannot be explained on this premise since sometimes one and sometimes the other is more accurate in incorporating Mark. In the same vein no clear priority can be established between Matthew and Luke with reference to the material common only to them. Sometimes Matthew gives the impression of being the more primitive (Matt. 18:10–14 and parallel), but there are also instances when Matthew's version is more developed than Luke's version (again, the Lord's Prayer tradition, Luke 11:2–4 and parallel, is a good example).

B. The "Q" Hypothesis

That evidence compels us to consider the possibility of the existence of another source or sources besides the Gospel of Mark which provided additional Jesus stories for Matthew and Luke in their revision and expansion of the Markan narrative. Such an assumption has caused scholars to formulate the two source hypothesis. Although this hypothesis was first suggested about a century ago it received its classical description in English from B. H. Streeter in 1924.[25]

The hypothetical second source which the scholars conjectured to have been used by Matthew and Luke to supplement Mark has come to be called "Q." Although the origin of this designation is obscure it is generally assumed to have been derived from the German word *Quelle* (= source).[26]

It is possible to speak only of the probability of Q, for it is only a hypothesis. There are no existing ancient manuscripts or even manuscript fragments of such sources. Some scholars have sought to account for that remarkable lack by suggesting that Q was a document which ceased to circulate independently and fell into disuse in the early church once it had been incorporated into Matthew and Luke. But Mark was incorporated into Matthew and Luke, too. The analogy of the Gospel of Mark detracts from the persuasive force of that suggestion, for one could well ask why the same fate did not befall Mark. The difference may have been that the early church ultimately judged Mark as theologically orthodox while the community responsible for the Q traditions came to be regarded as heretical.

Even though Q is only a hypothesis it is a justifiable hypothesis, for such a conjecture best explains the evidence described above. It continues to influence New Testament study because, with modifications, it provides a viable basis for synoptic comparison. In other words, it works so well. As was the case with the Gospel of Mark so also is it appropriate for us now to observe that the use of Q by both Matthew and Luke is strong testimony to the high esteem in which it was held by important segments of the early church.

The two source hypothesis as we have so far described it may be diagrammed thus:

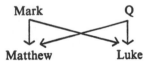

C. *Nature of Q*

Ambiguous and imprecise assumptions about the nature of Q have caused some confusion in New Testament studies. Scholars occasionally imply that Q was one single document. Other scholars employ Q simply as a symbol of convenience and include in it all of the material present in Matthew and Luke which is not in Mark. We need to modify both conceptions of Q.

Given the nature of the documents which do exist (our Synoptic Gospels), it simply is not possible for us to reconstruct the exact contents of Q. We see how tentative any attempt to recover the written text of Q must necessarily be by considering that if the Gospel of Mark did not exist we would be able to reconstruct from Matthew and Luke only a little more than half of his document. Further, it would be very difficult if not impossible for us to distinguish Markan material from Q material. Finally, we would find it very hard to recover and restore the exact Markan wording freed from the changes and adaptations which Luke and Matthew imposed.

Is there any way that we can identify when Matthew and Luke were both using the same second written document (besides Mark's Gospel)? In those traditions which evidence almost word for word vocabulary agreement (e.g., Matt. 3:7–10 and Luke 3:7–9), the probability that the source is a written document is very high. When the degree of vocabulary similarity diverges widely (e.g., Matt. 5:3–12 and Luke 6:20–23) we may suspect that either Matthew or Luke or both might have drastically modified a common written source. But we must also consider the alternate possibility that Matthew and Luke have incorporated the same tradition as it was transmitted to them through two different cycles of the oral tradition. An oral culture remembers traditions, especially brief, stereotyped proverbs and sayings, with sometimes astounding accuracy of detail.[27] It seems best for us to think of Q as including one or more written documents and, in addition, some Jesus traditions current in multiple strata of the oral tradition.

We will want to nuance the hypothesis of the Q source with some further qualifications. From the way Matthew and Luke used the Gospel of Mark (see chapters 3 and 4) it is probable that some of the written portions of Q were only used by one and not the other. When that has happened we can identify the tradition as belonging to Q solely on the basis of a similar, distinct theology. Such an identification becomes vastly more tentative—actually undemonstrable.

Further, there are a few times when Matthew and Luke have a tradition whose same general features are in Mark, but which differs enough in detail from Mark's version to indicate that it has come from a different source. Such instances probably reflect a similar tradition present in both Mark and written Q. Ordinarily Luke tended to prefer the Q version while Matthew conflated the details from both sources and produced a composite. (Examples are the John the Baptist material—Luke 3:1–9 and parallels, and the temptation traditions—Luke 4:1–13 and parallels.)

On the basis of this observation we must allow a further possibility, although it cannot be verified. When either Matthew or Luke agrees to a substantial degree with the Markan version of a tradition over against the other Gospel, the divergent version may well have been part of Q.[28] Another inference stemming from our observations of the way Matthew and Luke used Mark is the suspicion that the order of the Q written material is probably better preserved in Luke, and with less editing, than in Matthew. This is the reason why scholars usually refer to Q traditions by citing the Lukan passage rather than the widely scattered Matthean parallels. All subsequent statements we will make about the nature, contents, and theological interests of Q are modified by the above considerations.

D. The Contents of Q

The traditions in Matthew and Luke which scholars most frequently assign to the Q source consist primarily of speeches and sayings attributed to Jesus. The main exceptions they make are also to include brief references to John the Baptist (nos. 1, 9, 10, below), the temptation tradition (no. 2, below) and the story of the centurion at Capernaum (no. 8, below). Matthew and Luke regularly recorded the same saying of Jesus in different contexts, so we may conclude that Q was a collection of sayings of Jesus[29] without any narrative description of the circumstances surrounding the saying.

Since Q presumably contained no Passion narrative and, indeed, seemed to lack any reference to the cross event, we should not think of it as a Gospel but rather as a collection of miscellaneous "logia" (words, sayings) arranged topically. The material reported the teaching and preaching of Jesus. It was used by Matthew and Luke to augment Mark's narrative which had placed greater emphasis on the mighty acts and miraculous deeds of Jesus than on his teachings. We may group the kinds of sayings contained in Q into three divisions: eschatological (end-time) sayings, prophecies, and wisdom traditions.[30]

Guide to the Contents of Q[31]

	Luke	Matthew	(Mark)
1. The Preaching of John	3:7–9	3:7–10	1:7–8
	3:15–18	3:11–12	
2. Temptations	4:1–13	4:1–11	
3. Beatitudes	6:20b–23	5:3–12	
4. Love of Enemies	6:27–36	5:38–48	
		7:12	
5. Judging	6:37–42	7:1–5	4:24–25
		12:36–37	
		15:14	
		10:24–25	
6. Fruits	6:43–45	7:15–20	
		12:33–35	
7. House on Rock	6:46–49	7:21–27	
8. Centurion of Capernaum	7:1–10	8:5–13	
	13:28–29		
9. John's Question and Jesus' Answer	7:18–23	11:2–6	
10. Jesus' Witness to John	7:24–35	11:7–19	
	16:16	21:31–32	
11. Commissioning the Twelve	9:1–6	10:1	6:6b–13
		10:7–11	
		10:14	
12. On Following Jesus	9:57–62	8:18–22	
13. Commissioning of 70	10:1–12	9:37–38	
		10:7–16	
14. Woes on Galilee	10:13–15	11:20–24	
	10:12		
15. Whoever Hears You, Hears Me	10:16	10:40	
16. Thanksgiving and Blessedness of Disciples	10:21–24	11:25–27	
		13:16–17	
17. Lord's Prayer	11:1–4	6:9–13	
18. Encouragement to Pray	11:9–13	7:7–11	
19. Beelzebul Controversy	11:14–23	12:22–30	3:22–27
		9:32–34	
20. Return of the Evil Spirit	11:24–26	12:43–45	
21. Sign of Jonah	11:16	12:38–42	8:11–12
	11:29–32	16:1–4	

22. Sound Eye	11:34–36	6:22–23	
23. Against the Pharisees	11:37–54	23:4–36	7:1–9
24. Fearless Confession	12:2–9	10:26–33	
25. Sin against the Holy Spirit	12:10	12:31–32	3:29–30
26. Assistance of the Holy Spirit	12:11–12	10:19–20	13:11
	21:14–15		
27. Anxiety	12:22–32	6:25–34	
28. Treasures in Heaven	12:33–34	6:19–21	
29. Watchfulness and Faithfulness	12:35–48	24:42–51	
30. Divisions in Households	12:49–53	10:34–36	
31. Signs of the Times	12:54–56	16:2–3	
32. Agreement with Accuser	12:57–59	5:25–26	
33. Mustard Seed	13:18–19	13:31–32	4:30–32
34. Leaven	13:20–21	13:33	
35. Exclusion from the Kingdom	13:22–30	7:13–14	
		7:22–23	
		8:11–12	
		19:30	
36. Lament over Jerusalem	13:34–35	23:37–39	
37. Great Supper	14:15–24	22:1–14	
38. Conditions of Discipleship	14:25–33	10:37–38	
39. Parable of Salt	14:34–35	5:13	9:49–50
40. Lost Sheep	15:1–7	18:12–14	
41. Two Masters	16:13	6:24	
42. Concerning the Law	16:16–17	11:12–13	
		5:18	
43. Warning against Offenses	17:1–3a	18:6–7	9:42
44. On Forgiveness	17:3b–4	18:15	
		18:21–22	
45. On Faith	17:5–6	17:19–20	9:28–29
46. Day of the Son of Man	17:22–37	24:23	13:19–23
		24:26–27	13:14–16
		24:37–39	
		24:17–18	
		10:39	
		24:40–41	
		24:28	
47. Parable of Pounds	19:11–27	25:14–30	
48. Precedence	22:28–30	19:28	10:41–45

When we glance over the column of Q traditions in the Gospel of Luke (the first column), we can see Luke's typical manner of incorporating material from his sources in blocks. The main blocks of Q material in Luke (which also include some additions from sources other than Q) are Luke 3:7—4:13 (nos. 1 and 2, above); 6:20—7:35 (nos. 3–10); 9:57—10:24 (nos. 12–16); 11—12:59 (nos. 17–32); 13: 18–35 (nos. 33–36); 14:15—15:7 (nos. 37–40); 17:1–37 (nos. 43–46). Luke scattered a few isolated brief Q traditions elsewhere, and that accounts for the numbered sections in the list that are not included in one of the larger blocks.

By comparison we can also see how Matthew was more inclined to divide his source material into small fragments. Then he fundamentally reordered them before incorporating them into his narrative sequence. As we will see in the next chapter he did something similar with the Gospel of Mark. That is why scholars depend on Luke's arrangement to reflect more closely the sequence of traditions in Q. "Of special importance here is Vincent Taylor's article on the order of Q in which he shows that Luke's arrangement is usually followed by Matthew *if* we look independently at each of Matthew's five collections of sayings material."[32] (Matt. 5—7; 10; 13; 18; 23—25).

E. The Theology of Q

We do not know if Matthew and Luke included all of the Q material into their Gospels. There may well have been some sayings of Jesus or other stories about Jesus in the Q tradition which both Gospel writers left out. If we assume that the Q materials which we can recover from Matthew and Luke are characteristic of that tradition then several striking aspects of the theology of Q become apparent.

The Q tradition did not seem to be so concerned to give direct answers to the Jesus question. The identity of Jesus was not a major interest. Q stories employed only a few christological titles. None of them were developed extensively (the sayings which concern the future Son of man figure come the closest to expressing a developed doctrine of Christ).

We are surprised to realize that the Q material said very little about the fate of Jesus. Although his death and resurrection came to stand at the very center of the Christian faith for most early Christians, those events are not mentioned in the Q traditions. As far as we can tell there was no Passion narrative in Q, either. We must remind ourselves, however, that Luke knew a Passion narrative tradition that was different from Mark's (which Matthew followed). Maybe Luke found it in Q. Q had no developed theology of the saving nature of Jesus' death. Actually, we find very little of that kind of theological reflection in the Gospel of Luke, either. Those similarities are interesting but we must not push them too far.

Edwards has described the community responsible for the accumulation of the Q tradition and the composition of the written portions of that tradition as a self-sustaining group within early Christianity which:

1. anticipated the imminent return of Jesus as the Son of man,
2. continued to preach the proclamation of Jesus by repeating his sayings,
3. considered Jesus still active within the community through the inspiration of Christian prophets who spoke in his name,
4. was engaged in preparing for his coming by fulfilling the demands placed upon them by the coming judge,
5. was conscious of the negative reaction which could result in persecution for those who spoke and acted as Jesus commanded them.[33]

The community from which Q emerged was a Christian community. Although there is no Passion narrative the Q traditions presuppose belief in the Easter message as God's vindication of Jesus' life, ministry, and message. The community continued the preaching of Jesus in its own preaching, because Jesus' proclamation had been divinely validated and confirmed through the resurrection. Its collection of Jesus traditions reflects emphasis upon the impending inbreaking of the kingly rule of God. The sayings of Jesus were considered to have an enduring relevance which extended into the present time of the Q community. Consequently its proclamation primarily repeated the proclamation of Jesus.

The Jesus sayings of the Q traditions included wisdom and prophetic as well as eschatological (end-time) sayings. The three types of

sayings were interwoven so that the eschatological type was dominant. The Q community saturated its preaching of the message of
Jesus with a sense of the urgent necessity to respond decisively to the
offer of God's salvation. Hearers who accepted that preaching had to
prepare with single-mindedness for the coming of Jesus as Son of man,
the judge of the end of the world.

F. Locating the Community

For a considerable period of time New Testament scholarship
naively assumed that early Christianity developed as a single, solitary
major religious movement. Only insignificant splinter groups broke
away to pursue an independent (and presumably defective) course for
short-lived periods. Recently voices have been raised to remind us of
the remarkable variety of vigorous alternative responses to the Easter
faith which thrived concurrently for a considerable period in the
development of early Christianity.[34]

Only gradually did an "orthodoxy" (a system of authorized beliefs) develop. This orthodox faith of the great church was increasingly jealous of in-house aberrations as it became more solidly
entrenched, accepted, and established. The community which was
responsible for Q may well have embodied such an alternate response
to the Easter message. If so, it probably was more and more suppressed as that segment of Christianity which concentrated on the
proclamation of Jesus himself as the end-time, suffering, salvation
bringer came into the ascendancy.

We must assume that the two evangelists who composed the
Gospels of Matthew and Luke valued highly the Jesus traditions
preserved by the community of Q but did not concur with its theological views, or, more precisely, the focus of its missionary message.
They took the Q traditions and incorporated them into the Markan
narrative framework which had as its climactic moment the cross
event. They were thereby contributing to the process of conforming
a deviant theological perspective to that of emerging main-stream
Christianity.

It is also possible, indeed, probable, that the variety of Christianity
represented by Q continued to prosper alongside a strain of Christian-

ity which focused on the cross event. Ultimately such a tradition may well have contributed to the exclusive emphasis on the sayings of Jesus which we can observe in the documents of second and third century gnostic Christianity such as the Gospel of Thomas.

The time and place for the accumulation of the Q traditions and the composition of its written parts is very uncertain. Scholars have proposed tentative dates extending from the forties into the seventies of the first century, C.E. Jerusalem, Northern Palestine, and Syrian Antioch are all defensible guesses for the provenance of Q. It is unlikely that these matters will ever be more certainly known.

CHAPTER THREE
Why Expand a Gospel?
The Gospel of Matthew

The Gospel of Matthew is the first book in the New Testament. Historically it has been held in the highest favor by the church. This is partially because it includes more of the traditions about the life and teaching of Jesus than do the other Gospels in the Bible. It was also thought to be the earliest of the Gospels since it was believed to have been composed by Matthew Levi, one of the Twelve who were intimate associates of Jesus during his ministry. Only recently has this view of the authorship of the Gospel of Matthew been abandoned by most scholars. We will discuss why that view is no longer held later.

This chapter will describe some characteristic features of the Gospel of Matthew, search out the literary structure of the document, consider those theological interests and purposes which evidently motivated Matthew's writing, examine the nature of the Christian community for which the work was composed, review what can be known about the author, and give an outline of the contents of the book.

I. CHARACTERISTIC TRAITS OF MATTHEW

A. Matthew's Use of Christian Sources

1. Mark

An assumption of the two-source hypothesis[1] is that Matthew had a copy of Mark before him which he used to compose his Gospel. As an extension of that assumption, most scholars simply presume that Mark's Gospel was also known by the Christian community to which Matthew belonged. It had used the Gospel of Mark in its worship, its catechetical teaching (its oral religious instruction) and its missionary preaching. It had used Mark's Gospel for a long enough period of time to know well the value of that document. But Matthew had also recognized some of its inadequacies in helping his community to respond to the challenges, opportunities, and attacks with which it was trying to cope. The burning issues with which Matthew and his community were struggling were simply not identical with those which had concerned Mark and his church.

When Matthew is compared with Mark, many of the changes which Matthew made in Mark's narrative are obvious. Those changes provide important clues to help identify the differences in the historical life settings of the Markan and Matthean communities. They also disclose some of the unique qualities which Matthew possessed as an author.

The artistry with which Matthew combined and organized the traditions which he gathered from a number of different sources was extraordinary. In the process he also molded that traditional material so that it strengthened the faith of the Christian community to which he belonged, supporting it as it struggled with specific issues related to its life and work.

The Gospel of Mark provided the basic narrative framework for Matthew. But he expanded it and reworked it. Matthew's revisions of Mark included alterations in detail, condensations, and new formulations. The result was both abbreviation and improvement of the literary quality of Mark's narrative. What was subtracted in narrative content was more than replaced by the extensive additions of traditions about Jesus which Matthew included beyond what Mark had used.

Matthew corrected Mark's Greek considerably. Mark was addicted to the use of the present tense. (He wrote the story of Jesus as a child talks: "He comes to the house and gets us and we go to school.") Matthew usually altered such "historical present tenses" (130 of 151 times). In the account of the healing of the paralytic, Matthew replaced Mark's rather crude Greek word for "pallet" (Mark 2:4) with the more polished word for "bed" (Matt. 9:2). Mark's imprecise reference to "King Herod" (Mark 6:14) was corrected by Matthew to "Herod, the tetrarch" (Matt. 14:1).

Where Mark was unnecessarily repititious:

> That evening, at sundown, they brought to him all who were sick or possessed with demons. . . . And he healed many who were sick with various diseases, and cast out many demons. (Mark 1:32–34a)

Matthew was more concise and vivid:

> That evening they brought to him many who were possessed with demons; and he cast out the spirits with a word, and healed all who were sick. (Matt. 8:16)

By altering the connective links between scenes in the story of Jesus, Matthew considerably improved the narrative flow, increasing the sense of chronological sequence and spatial relation. Matthew's "While he was still speaking to the people . . ." (Matt. 12:46) is much more effective than Mark's "And . . ." (Mark 3:31). So is "That same day Jesus went out of the house and sat beside the sea . . ." (Matt. 13:1) in place of "Again he began to teach beside the sea . . ." (Mark 4:1).

2. "Q"

The Gospel of Mark was not the only source which Matthew used in writing his Gospel. He also drew upon those traditions about Jesus which had been collected in the source or sources commonly designated "Q."[2] As we noted earlier it is impossible to reconstruct the contents of that source in precise detail.[3] Nevertheless we may assume that Matthew reworked, revised, corrected, and adapted the material he selected from Q in a manner similar to the way he made use of Mark's traditions. It is interesting to note that the author of Matthew was not the only one who valued the material in Q. Luke also saw its importance and made extensive use of it when he revised Mark's Gospel, too. It is strange that a document such as Q which was so highly esteemed by early Christians did not survive except for its traces discernible in Matthew and in Luke.

3. "M"

When the material from Mark and the Q traditions are combined they still don't produce the Gospel of Matthew in its entirety. There are around 400 verses or verse fragments in Matthew that are not present in either Mark or Q. They are exclusive to Matthew and are not found anywhere else in the New Testament. Where did they come from?

Although some scholars have wanted to propose a third written document they have not been able to agree on what out of Matthew's special material should be included in it. The evidence and the controls which govern any theory of literary dependency simply aren't present. With the possible exceptions of the genealogy (Matt. 1:2–17) and the "testimony traditions,"[4] it is more probable that Matthew's special material was drawn from the oral traditions still circulating among early Christians. The possibility that Matthew occasionally may have composed an entire pericope can be neither excluded or established.

Besides the genealogy Matthew's special material includes the birth and infancy stories (Matt. 1—2). Unlike Luke's nativity narratives which stress the dimension of the miraculous in the conception and birth of Jesus, Matthew's infancy narratives emphasize the identity of Jesus. That is particularly evident with the description of the name given to him by God (Matt. 1:21–25). It also is implied in the journey narrative from Bethlehem to Nazareth by way of Egypt (Matt. 2:1–23; this passage includes the tradition of the "Wise Men" so familiar to us during the Christmas and Epiphany seasons).

Other special Matthean material includes the appearances of Jesus after the resurrection (Matt. 28), a notable number of quotations from the Jewish Scriptures which he understood as referring to incidents in Jesus' life, and a large amount of the sayings and teachings of Jesus, most of which are included in the five great discourses.[5] Also some narrative accounts such as the coin in the fish's mouth (Matt. 17: 24–27), the suicide of Judas (Matt. 27:3–10),[6] the dream of Pilate's wife (Matt. 27:19), the guard at the tomb (Matt. 27:62–66, 28:4).[7]

Even though it is not possible to establish that Matthew drew his special material from a single document these traditions are usually represented by the letter "M." In this way we can refer to them as a group and more easily distinguish them from the traditions Matthew adapted from Mark and Q. The diagram showing the literary relationships of the Synoptic Gospels and the sources they used, begun on page 85, may be completed for Matthew as follows:

It is worth repeating again that neither M nor Q necessarily represents a single document.

4. Effect of Revisions

Mark wrote the story of Jesus to evoke stronger faith in those who read it. It was a narrative "sermon." If Mark wanted to preach, by contrast, Matthew wanted to teach. This contrast should not be pushed too far but rather regarded as an indication of differing emphases. Mark certainly also wanted to teach his community more about Jesus and the Easter faith, and Matthew was also eager that his community's faith be more intense as well as better informed.

Whereas Mark gave prominence to the marvelous deeds of Jesus, Matthew inserted a large amount of Jesus logia (words, sayings) traditions from Q and M. He organized and systematized the material around central themes. Greater importance was thereby given to the teachings of Jesus.

Matthew took over the motif of "greater authority" which Mark had used to describe the power of Jesus. His authority to overcome the forces of evil opposed to God far surpassed the authority of the religious leaders. Matthew made this "greater authority" motif a repetitive refrain which distinguished the teachings of Jesus from rabbinical instruction. Jesus taught with greater authority than did the scribes and Pharisees. This implied that anyone whose teaching conformed to the teaching of Jesus (i.e., Matthew and his community) taught with greater authority than did those who stood in continuity with the scribes and Pharisees (i.e., rabbinic Judaism).

Matthew greatly expanded Mark's section of special instruction by Jesus to the disciples. The "privacy" of the instruction was not intended to claim that it was to be kept secret. Rather, for the Easter community, that instruction was precisely the source, rightly interpreted, of their public proclamation.

He also did something that is quite significant with the story of Jesus as a whole. He lengthened it by making changes at both ends. By extending Mark's story framework both backwards (genealogy, infancy stories) and forwards (empty tomb account, appearances of the risen Messiah), Matthew altered the nature of the narrative. No longer are we left abruptly before the scene of the empty tomb, as Mark left us, faced with the demand to decide how we will respond. What for Mark was present proclamation becomes a record of past events in the Gospel of Matthew. A historicizing tendency has been introduced. The story of Jesus does not continue on without interruption into the story of the believing church. The time of Jesus is a special kind of time. It is the time of the fulfillment of that salvation for which the fathers and the prophets prepared. It is also time distinct from the time of the church whose existence is anticipated (Matt. 16:18) but not actually inaugurated until the time of Jesus was completed (Matt. 28:19–20).

B. Matthew's Use of the Jewish Scriptures

1. Frequency and Method

A conspicuous feature of Matthew's Gospel is his extensive use of citations and allusions to the religious traditions recorded in the Jewish Scriptures. That is not to imply that Mark was not dependent on Old Testament traditions, too. He was. However, even in proportion to the greater length of his Gospel, Matthew employed them much more frequently. He creatively combined two major religious traditions which were valued by early Christians: the Jewish Scriptures and the stories about Jesus.

It is likely that Matthew wrote his Gospel in Greek. Matthew's use of Mark and the written portions of Q, both of which were in the Greek language, indicates this. Although he frequently cited texts from the Greek translation of the Jewish Scriptures (the Septuagint), he knew them in the original Hebrew, and on occasion preferred his own translation. The fact that Matthew knew Greek does not imply that he was not a Jewish Christian. Remember that Paul wrote in Greek and quoted from the Septuagint, yet he was certainly a Jew.

Matthew assumed that his audience was familiar with the Jewish Scriptures. (He also assumed familiarity with Jewish customs and expressions, Jewish oral tradition, and rabbinical interpretation.) His argument sometimes depended on the ability of his hearers to consider the broader Old Testament context in which the texts he cited originally appeared.[8]

The methods Matthew applied to accommodate incidents in the Jesus story to Old Testament texts sometimes perplex and even trouble us. His search for an appropriate passage that would conform to an event in the Jesus tradition sometimes led him to quote a passage without regard for its context. "Out of Egypt have I called my son," which Matthew (2:15) applied to the flight of Mary, Joseph, and Jesus to Egypt, described originally, in Hosea, the Exodus deliverance of Israel from Egyptian slavery (Hos. 11:1). Jeremiah's lament for an Israel herded away to exile (Jer. 31:15) is converted into anticipation of the grief caused by Herod's murder of the male children of Bethlehem (Matt. 2:16–18).

Occasionally Matthew appeals to a Jewish tradition text in such a vague way that the Scripture he had in mind is uncertain, at least to us.

"And he went and dwelt in a city called Nazareth, that *what was spoken by the prophets* might be fulfilled, 'He shall be called a Nazarene' " (Matt. 2:23, italics added). The text that Matthew was citing in that instance is obscure. Maybe he intended a word-play on the Hebrew word for "root" in Isaiah 11:1. Maybe he was alluding to "the boy shall be a Nazarite" of Judges 13:5. Either possibility is remote.

The Old Testament mentions neither the village of Nazareth nor the term for its inhabitants.

There are instances where Matthew modified a particular Jesus tradition so that it conformed to a text from the Hebrew Scriptures. He added additional travel itinerary to Mark's version of Jesus' arrival in Galilee in order to make the trip correspond to a prophecy from Isaiah (Matt. 4:12–16; compare Mark 1:14). Similarly the general term "the money" which Judas received from the Temple officials for betraying Jesus becomes exactly "thirty pieces of silver" only in Matthew (Matt. 26:14–15; compare Mark 14:10–11; Luke 22:3–5) so that the conformity of the amount of money to Zechariah 11:12–13[9] is precise (Matt. 27:9).

In contrast to the freedom with which Matthew often combined the narrative of Jesus and the Jewish traditions he occasionally went to the opposite extreme. A bent toward literalism produced Matthew's strange alteration of Mark's description of Jesus' entry into Jerusalem. Matthew described Jesus as riding on *two* animals (Matt. 21:7; compare Mark 11:7) because of the double expression in the Old Testament text:

> Lo, your king comes to you;
> . . . .
> humble and riding on an ass,
>   *on a colt* the foal of an ass. (Zech. 9:9, italics added)

Such a flagrant disregard of typical Hebrew parallelism (the same thing being said with two different expressions) has caused skepticism about Matthew's Jewish background. Yet rabbinical literature amply testifies that not only extreme literalism but also all of the other interpretive methods Matthew employed with Jewish Scripture were common rabbinic exegetical devices. Such methods were devised to restore interpretive flexibility to ancient texts which had been relevant when they were first written but whose significance had become remote.

2. Formula Quotations

The frequent use of stereotyped, "promise and fulfillment" formulae to introduce quotations from the Jewish Scriptures is a distinctive feature of the Gospel of Matthew. The characteristic form of the formula runs: "such and such an event in the life of Jesus took place in order to fulfill what the prophet had said." There are twelve of these quotations: Matt. 1:22–23; 2:5–6, 15, 17–18, 23; 4:14–16; 8:17; 12:17–21; 13:14–15, 35; 21:4–5; 27:9–10 (cf. also 3:3–4; 11:10; 15:7–9; 26:56).

Matthew emphasized the rhythm of "promise-fulfillment" in his rewriting of the story of Jesus to stress that God achieved in Jesus those saving purposes which he had revealed in the Jewish Scriptures. The tremendous authority which the Jewish Scriptures carried was thereby passed to the person and work of Jesus. The Scriptures provided proof of the religious meaning of events in Jesus' life.

Such a use of the Jewish Scriptures was serviceable particularly in the Christian mission to the Jews. Matthew probably adopted and intensified a manner of argument that had been developed much earlier in the Christian missionary preaching tradition.[10]

The "promise-fulfillment" pattern also contributed to the historicizing process which Matthew imposed upon the Markan narrative. The special time of Jesus is the time of the awaited Messiah of the Jewish Scriptures.

C. Organization of Jesus Traditions

1. Topical Groupings

As Matthew accumulated the traditions about Jesus from different sources (Mark, Q, M), he usually divided them into individual traditions. This was particularly the case with the teaching traditions. By way of exception he preserved the narrative skeleton of Mark.

In reconstructing the story of Jesus he gathered the traditions into topical or subject groups. One way he organized material was by grouping it together and including it in his Gospel at those places which the content indicated was appropriate (infancy stories, Passion narratives, post-resurrection accounts). Other collections seem to have been gathered with respect to the types of the stories (miracle stories—Matt. 8—9; parables—Matt. 13). A third variety was determined by the topical content of the Jesus teachings.

We can observe how Matthew did this by looking at five relatively large blocks of material. These five accumulations of Jesus' teachings traditionally have been called the great discourses. A discourse is a formal discussion of a subject. In each case he organized the material according to topic. The third discourse listed below was organized both by topic (the kingdom of heaven) and by type of story (parables).

1) Sermon on the Mount (Matt. 5—7)
2) Discourse on Mission (Matt. 10)
3) Parables of the Kingdom of Heaven (Matt. 13)
4) Discourse on Church Discipline (Matt. 18)
5) Discourse on End-Time Judgment (Matt. 23—25)

Matthew apparently obtained the core of the first discourse from Q. We know this because of the very similar material which is in Luke (Luke 6:20–49) but not in Mark. On the other hand, we find that the nucleus of the other four came from Mark (Matt. 10 and Mark 3:13–19; 6:8–11; Matt. 13 and Mark 4; Matt. 18 and Mark 9:33–50; Matt. 23—25 and Mark 13). By comparing each passage in Matthew with the corresponding passage in Mark and noting the differences we are able to observe Matthew's method of revising and expanding Mark.

In addition to the five great discourses Matthew included other, briefer discourses in his Gospel. The speech by John the Baptist (Matt. 3:7–12) or the Great Commission discourse (Matt. 28:18–20) are examples.

The smaller speeches are different from the five great discourses, however, because they don't end in the same way. Each of the five major speeches concludes with a stereotyped formula. "And when Jesus finished these sayings [or 'instructing,' or 'parables'] . . ." occurs as a redactional conclusion and transition at Matt. 7:28–29; 11:1; 13:53–54; 19:1; 26:1. Matthew likely intended to suggest through the five-discourses device a correlation between the teaching of Jesus and the Mosaic Law.[11] Jesus' teaching fulfills the Law of Moses (Matt. 5:17–20).[12]

2. Development of Ideas

Matthew provided additional coherence for his Gospel by repeating the same themes at regular intervals in the narrative. He intentionally wove and interlocked ideas. As we can observe by reading

Thematic Correlations Between Various Sections Within Matthew's Gospel (*Interlocking ideas*)

Ch. 1-4	5-7	8-9	10	11-12	13	14-17	18	19-22	23-25	26-28

```
3:15 ━ 5:20 ━ Fulfill All Righteousness
       7:28f ━ 9:33f ━━━━━━━━━━━━━━13:8,24,47 ━━━ Dual Reaction
       7:29 ━ 8:9 ┓━ 10:1 ━━━━━━━━━━ Authority ━━━━━━━━━━ 21:23 ━━━━━━━━━━ 28:18
               9:6, 8┘                                              ┏━━ 23:34
       5:11 ━━━━━━━━━ 10:18 ━━━━━━━ 13:21 ━ Suffer for Christ's Sake ┫ 24:9
3:3 ┓━━━━━ 8:17 ━━━━━━━ 11:2-5 ┓━13:14 ━ 15:7 ━ Prophecy of Isaiah
4:14┘                  12:17 ┘ 13:21  ┏15:12
               Offense 11:6 ┓━13:57 ━┛17:27 ━ 18:6 ━━━━━━━ 24:10 ━ 26:31
                       ┏8:10       ┏15:28
       Faith ┫9:2,22,29        ┗17:20 ━ 21:21 ━━━━━━━━━ 23:23
               8:11f ━ Gentiles in Kingdom of Heaven ━━━━━ 21:43
3:7 ━━━ 5:20  Condemns Pharisees 12:7 ━━━━━━━┏15:3 ━━━━━━ 21:45 ━ 23
                                          ┗16:12
3:7 ━ Brood of Vipers ━━━━━━ 12:34 ━━━━━━━━━━━━━━━━━━━━━ 23:33
1:24┓                              14:29
3:15┫━ 7:21 ━ 9:9 ━━━━━━━ 12:50 ━━━━━ 15:6 ┫━ Acts of Obedience ━━ 26:39f
4:19┛                              17:5
4:23 ━━━━━━━ 9:35 ━ Gospel of the Kingdom ━━●━━━━━━━━━━ 24:14 ━ 26:13
               Imminence of Kingdom ━ 16:28 ━━━━━━━━━━━ 24:34
3:1┓                               ┏14:2f
4:12┫John ━━ 9:14 ━━━━━ 11:2-18 ━━┫16:14 ━━━━━ 21:25-32
                                  ┗17:13
       Both Good & Bad Included 13:47 ━━━━━━━━━━ 22:10
       6:14f ━━━━━━━━ Forgive to Be Forgiven ━━━━━━ 18:35
```

Verbal Correlations Within Matthew's Gospel (*Interlocking quotes*)

```
4:23 ━━━━━━ 9:35 ━ Summary
3:2 ┓━━━━━━━━━━━━━ 10:7 ━ Kingdom of Heaven at Hand
4:17┛
3:10 ━ 7:19 ━━━━━━━━━━━━━ 12:33ff ━ Good Tree—Good Fruit
4:24 ━ Fame—Brought Him All Sick ━━━━━━━━━ 14:35
3:17 ━ Voice: This Is My beloved Son ━━━━━━━ 17:5
       5:29 ━ Right Eye Cause to Sin—Pluck Out ━━━ 18:9
       5:32 ━ Divorce and Remarry—Adultery ━━━━━━━ 19:9
       5:18 ━ Heaven and Earth Pass Away, Law/My Word Not Pass Away 24:35
       7:28 ━ Formula ━━━━ 11:1 ━ 13:53 ━━━━━━ 19:1 ━━━━━━ 26:1
       9:13 ━━━━━━━ 12:7 ━ Mercy, Not Sacrifice
       9:34 ━━━━━━━ 12:24 ━ Alliance with Demons
       9:20 ━━━━━━━━━━━━━━━━ 14:36 ━ Touch Garment Fringe—Made Well
               10:6 ━━━━━━━ 15:24 ━ To Lost Sheep of House of Israel
               10:38f ━━━━━━ 16:24f ━ Take Cross, Follow Me
               10:22 ━ Hated by All ... for My Name's Sake ━ 24:9
               10:22 ━ But He Who Endures to the End Will Be ━ 24:13 ━ Saved
               10:40ff ━ Receive X—Receive Me ━ 18:5 ━━━━━━ 25:40
               12:38f ━━━━━━ 16:1,2,4, Sign of Jonah
To One Who Has More Will Be Given ━ 13:12 ━━━━━━━━━━━ 25:29
               Blind/Loose 16:19 ━ 18:18
               Faith—Move Mountains 17:20f ━━━━ 21:21
               Great—Servant 18:1 ━ 20:26f ━ 23:11
                       First—Last ┏19:30
                                  ┗20:16
               Blest He Who Comes ━ 21:9 ━ 23:39
               Held John/Jesus a Prophet ┏21:26
                                         ┗21:46
```

through the Gospel this provides a strong sense of continuity and theological harmony. One scholar has charted the recurrence of some Matthean ideas like this:[13]

The repetition of themes was one way ancient writers emphasized important ideas. The literary device also helped them guide their listeners to a deeper and more profound understanding. The reiteration of motifs has the effect of developing a progressively complex understanding of the themes. Clarity is attained by degrees. The full meaning of the idea is accessible when the significance of each of its uses is added together. Only when the theme has been traced all the way through the Gospel is the hearer able to appreciate its full intensity and depth wherever it occurs.[14]

The way in which Matthew developed the idea of authority is a good example of his use of repetition. At the end of the Gospel the transfer of authority by Jesus to his disciples occurs. "All authority in heaven and on earth has been given to me. Go therefore and make disciples . . . baptizing . . . teaching" (Matt. 28:18–20). The use of the idea of authority in this passage gathers together and assumes knowledge of each of the previous uses of that idea as it related both to Jesus (Matt. 5:17–48; 7:28–29; 8:27; 9:6–8, 34; 11:27; 12:23–32; 13:41–42; 21:23–27; 25:31–33) and to the disciples (Matt. 10:1, 24–25, 40; 13:52; 17:16–20; 18:18–20; 19:28–30; 20:21–28; 23:8–12, 34). The Great Commission anticipates the time when the church teaches and ministers with a supernatural authority second only to Jesus'. Their authority is greater than that of the rabbis.

The cumulative effect which the repetition of ideas has moves in both directions, however. The force of all of the authority passages listed above converges in the Great Commission. But they also explain and elaborate every other use of the authority. So they all clarify and contribute to our understanding of what Matthew was saying about Jesus when he wrote "the crowds were astonished at his teaching, for he taught them as one who had authority, and not as their scribes" (Matt. 7:28–29). Although this passage relating the idea of authority to Jesus occurs early in the Gospel of Matthew we have not fully understood it until we read it in the light of all other Matthean passages which speak of authority including the Great Commission. This is but one example of the way Matthew developed his ideas.[15]

D. Other Distinctive Features

1. Miracle Stories Modified

Matthew gathered together the miracle stories he found in Mark and his other sources and concentrated many of them in one section of his Gospel (Matt. 8—9). In the process he usually altered the Markan versions by making them shorter and more compact. A comparison of the two versions of the exorcising of the demoniac(s) (Matt. 8:28–34 and Mark 5:1–17) or of the healing of the paralytic (Matt. 9:1–8 and Mark 2:1–12) vividly demonstrates Matthew's fondness for eliminating unnecessary words. His version usually sounds more dramatic and alive as a consequence.

The different ways that Matthew and Mark include miracle stories of Jesus in their narratives are interesting. Mark stressed miracle stories because they proclaimed the present establishment of God's kingly rule in the person of Jesus. He began his account of Jesus' ministry with several miracle stories (Mark 1:21—2:12). Matthew, however, was more interested in the portrait of Jesus as the authoritative interpreter of the will of God. He gathered together ten miracle stories into one section (Matt. 8—9). But he placed an extended section of teaching by Jesus before the collection of miracle stories— the Sermon on the Mount, the first major discourse (Matt. 5—7). By this means he subordinated the miracles to the teachings traditions. They were dramatic actualizations of those mighty supernatural deeds anticipated at the end of the world by the Jewish Scriptures (cf. Matt. 8:17). As Jesus' teachings authoritatively interpret the will of God so his deeds miraculously confirm his teachings.

The miracles collection in Matthew conform to the miraculous mighty acts which were expected at the end of time, the end of the world in its present form: "the blind receive their sight [Matt. 9:27–30] and the lame walk [cf. Matt. 9:2–7], lepers are cleansed [cf. Matt. 8:2–3] and the deaf hear [this one is lacking], and the dead are raised up [cf. Matt. 9:18–19, 23–25], and the poor have good news preached to them [by Jesus, Matt. 5—7; by the disciples, Matt. 10]" (Matt. 11:5; cf. Isa. 29:18–19; 35:5–6). Miracles play the role for Matthew of supporting and substantiating doctrine.

2. Knowledge of Jewish Customs Assumed

Matthew was confident that his community was well-informed about distinctively Jewish features in the Jesus traditions. This observation implies that a large part of the community either were Jewish Christians or had been exposed to Jewish culture and traditions for an extended period. Whereas Mark gave lengthy explanation about the Jewish cultic requirements for ritual washings (Mark 7:3–4), Matthew eliminated the explanation (Matt. 15:1–2). Apparently he felt most of his hearers would understand that. References to cultic cleansing (Matt. 23:25–26), to the Temple tax (Matt. 17:24–27), to phylacteries (leather cubes containing Scripture, worn during prayer) and to fringes on prayer shawls (Matt. 23:5) appear without further clarification. Matthew took it for granted that his hearers were familiar with excessive Pharisaic scrupulosity in observing the commandment to tithe (Matt. 23:23), and with the caricatures of ostentatious, arrogant, Jewish piety (Matt. 6:1–8; 23:6). The sharp sarcasm of Matthew 23:24 is clear only to those who know that both insects and camels were ritually unclean and therefore forbidden as food (cf. Lev. 11:4, 42–43). He assumed that a reference to the exaggerated eagerness of rabbinical Jews to win Gentile converts was clear (Matt. 23:15).

The way Mark described Jesus' teaching about divorce (Mark 10:1–12) was modified by Matthew to reflect the Jewish opinion that in the case of adultery only was divorce justified (Matt. 19:3–9). His version also conformed to the Jewish view that only the male partner could divorce. (Mark 10:12, reflecting the more liberal divorce customs of Greco-Roman society, was suppressed.) Furthermore, a very high valuation was placed by Matthew on the enduring validity of the Torah, the Jewish religious law (Matt. 5:17–19; 23:2–3).

Matthew's language also reflects a sympathetic awareness of Jewish practice. His modifications of the Lord's Prayer tradition (Matt. 6:9–15, cf. Luke 11:2–4) include typical Jewish liturgical features. Of the many times that the phrase "the kingdom of God" appeared in his sources Matthew changed all but four (Matt. 12:28; 19:24; 21:31, 43) to the phrase "the kingdom of heaven." Barclay called the phrase "a reverential periphrasis" which conforms to Jewish reluctance to use the actual name of God.[16]

3. Idealized Portraits

Matthew's reverent opinion of the person of Jesus and the role of the first disciples induced him to retouch some of the more human details in Mark's portrait of those persons. He intentionally altered Mark's description of Jesus. He suppressed details that suggested that Jesus was subject to human emotions. He also eliminated those parts of the traditions which expressed opinions about Jesus which Matthew considered insulting.

For example, in the account of the healing of a leper, Matthew omitted the note that Jesus was moved by pity (Matt. 8:2–3; cf. Mark 1:41). In the story in which the disciples prevented the children from being brought to Jesus, Matthew followed Mark's version in describing how Jesus blessed the children but avoided mentioning that Jesus was indignant at his disciples (Matt. 19:14; cf. Mark 10:14). Mark's report that some of Jesus' friends thought that he was crazy (Mark 3:21) was dropped by Matthew.

Similarly, some details of Mark's Gospel which showed the disciples in an unfavorable light were altered by Matthew to give a more complimentary impression. He softened Mark's suggestion that Jesus thought the disciples were dense (Matt. 13:16–18; cf. Mark 4:13; Matt. 14:33; cf. Mark 6:51–52). Matthew preferred to ascribe unseemly ambition to the mother of James and John rather than to the disciples themselves (Matt. 20:20; cf. Mark 10:35). These modifications are examples of Matthew's interest in idealizing the portrayals of his Gospel characters. Careful comparison of the two narratives will uncover other similar instances of Matthew's "corrective" revisions.

4. Use of Numbers

An intriguing feature of the Gospel of Matthew is its use of numbers. Matthew often arranged things numerically in twos, threes, fives, sevens. There are two demoniacs (Matt. 8:28), two blind men (Matt. 9:27; 20:30), two false witnesses (Matt. 26:60). Threefold groupings include the temptations (Matt. 4:1-11), examples of righteousness (Matt. 6:1–18), prohibitions (Matt.

6:19—7:6), commands (Matt. 7:7–20), miraculous healings (Matt. 8:1–15), miracles of power (Matt. 8:23—9:8), parables on sowing (Matt. 13:1–32), and frequently elsewhere. Besides the five major discourses[17] there are five illustrations of law fulfillment (Matt. 5:21–48). There are seven demons (Matt. 12:45), seven loaves and seven baskets (Matt. 15:34, 37), the sevenfold pardon (Matt. 18:21–22), seven brethren (Matt. 22:25), and seven "woes" (Matt. 23:13–30). The genealogy of Jesus divides into three groups of fourteen, or two times seven, names each (Matt. 1:2–17, see especially vs. 17).[18]

Such a use of numbers corresponds to the use of numerical devices in Jewish Scriptures and rabbinical traditions. It served a dual purpose: mnemonic—arranging of items in conveniently memorized groups, and aesthetic—incorporating pleasing symmetrical patterns into the narrative.

5. Use of "Church"

The Gospel of Matthew is the only Gospel in the Bible to make explicit use of the term "church" (Matt. 16:18; 18:17). The Hebrew equivalent for the term in the Jewish Scriptures referred to Israel who was the people of God. By his use of the term in his Gospel Matthew testified to his conviction that those whom Jesus saved (Matt. 1:21) now composed true Israel. It was distinct from Judaism though not necessarily exclusive of it.

II. STRUCTURE OF THE GOSPEL

We have seen that Matthew adopted the narrative skeleton of Mark as the framework for his own Gospel. To Mark's account he added a considerable amount of other Jesus traditions. But he did not simply combine his sources in an ill-considered, haphazard manner. He carefully ordered his material.

The most obvious indication of the care with which Matthew structured his Gospel are the discourses, the five major and the two minor ones. Although B. W. Bacon misinterpreted them as representing a new Pentateuch given by Jesus, the new Moses, his identification of the five major discourses as a significant structural component of Matthew was accurate.

Matthew combined the discourses with the narrative material in a fascinating way. The five major discourses are interspersed between the narrative sections. The two minor discourses are incorporated into the first and last narrative sections, and serve as oral interpretations of the narrative events in those sections. If we let N= narrative, D = major discourse and d = minor discourse we observe the following pattern: N(d)-D-N-D-N-D-N-D-N-D-N(d).[19] The major discourses are related to both of the narrative sections which bracket each of them. Matthew accomplished this through the repetition of themes,[20] the manner in which he made the concluding scene of the preceding narrative section introduce the next discourse and the stereotyped conclusions to the discourses with which he led into the next narrative section. Consequently the major discourses link two narrative sections together.

Matthew was not content with unfolding the story of Jesus in simple linear narrative sequence. He artfully composed his Gospel so that the alternating sections of narrative and discourse were interrelated in a chiasmus. "Chiasmus" is the name for a literary pattern in which elements are related to each other. The term comes from the observation that when the pattern is present in two lines (A–B; B¹–A¹) the relationship may be indicated by drawing an "x" (the Greek letter "chi") between them.

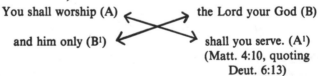

You shall worship (A)   the Lord your God (B)

and him only (B¹)   shall you serve. (A¹)
(Matt. 4:10, quoting
Deut. 6:13)

A and A¹ ("you shall worship" and "shall you serve") are synonymous expressions of the same religious attitude. B and B¹ ("the Lord your God" and "and him only") are synonymous references to the proper object of that religious attitude.

The center of a chiastic pattern usually contains the most significant elements in the pattern. In the example the references to God are in the position of most important emphasis. In order to demonstrate the place of emphasis in the chiastic pattern we may diagram the two lines in this manner:

A   You shall worship
　　B   the Lord your God
　　B¹　and him only
A¹   shall you serve

point of
emphasis

A chiasmus need not be limited to only two lines. It may well be extended over a long literary section or even an entire document. That is precisely what Matthew did. Chapter 13 (the discourse on the parables of the kingdom) is the center of the pattern.[21]

Chiastic Structure[22]

A. Narrative: Jesus as Messiah, Son of God (1—4)
　Minor discourse: John the Baptist identifies the authority of Jesus
　　　　　　　　　　　　　　　　　　　　　　　　(3:7–12)
　B. Discourse: Demands of true discipleship in end-time kingdom
　　　　　　　　　　　　　　　　　　　　　　　　(5—7)
　　C. Narrative: The miraculous supernatural authority of Jesus
　　　　　　　　　　　　　　　　　　　　　　　　(8—9)
　　　D. Discourse: Charge & authority of disciples (10)
　　　　E. Narrative: Jews reject Jesus (11—12)
　　　　　F. Discourse: Parables of the kingdom of heaven (13)
　　　　E.¹ Narrative: Disciples accept Jesus (14—17)
　　　D.¹ Discourse: Charge & authority of church (18)
　　C.¹ Narrative: Authority & invitation (19—22)
　B.¹ Discourse: End-time judgment on false discipleship (23—25)
A.¹ Narrative: Jesus as suffering and vindicated Messiah (26—28)
　Minor discourse: Jesus identifies the authority of the Church
　　　　　　　　　　　　　　　　　　　　　　　　(28:18–20)

Such an intricate balanced structure, besides providing literary cohesion and aesthetic pleasure, underscored a central theological idea that was crucial for Matthew. It contrasted the rejection of Jesus by historical Israel with his acceptance by the real Israel. Prior to chapter 13 Jesus' ministry was directed to the Jews who would not listen nor understand. After chapter 13 Jesus devoted himself to the disciples, the foundation generation of the church, who accepted him and believed in him.[23]

Matthew complemented the chiastic symmetry by intertwining a progressive disclosure of the riches of his christology (his doctrine of Christ). He signposted the stages of this development with the use of the phrase "From that time Jesus began. . . ." The phrase is used twice. It appears at Matthew 4:17 to signal the beginning of the public ministry of Jesus. Again it occurs at Matthew 16:21 to mark the beginning of a significant new dimension to the teaching of Jesus, his instructions to the disciples about his coming passion. Matthew thereby divided his affirmations about who Jesus was into three segments:[24]

   1) The person of Jesus Messiah (Matt. 1:1—4:16)
   2) The proclamation of Jesus Messiah (Matt. 4:17—16:20)
   3) The suffering, death, and resurrection of Jesus Messiah (Matt. 16:21—28:20)

With what brilliant artistry Matthew constructed the architectonic design of his Gospel!

III. WHY MATTHEW WROTE HIS GOSPEL

Matthew clearly had a great amount of admiration for what Mark had accomplished in writing his Gospel or he would not have used it as the basis for his own. He also shared that same strong conviction in the Easter faith which led Mark to compose his Gospel. Matthew had much in common with Mark.

Matthew would not have changed Mark's version of a particular tradition unless he thought that the changes improved the tradition and made it more effective. Neither would he have added more traditions to Mark unless he felt they enhanced and made more useful the Gospel narrative. It is to the changes and additions which Matthew made to Mark's Gospel that we look first in trying to discover what was of particular concern to him. There we discover indications of major interests and concerns Matthew had which he felt needed to be addressed more directly than the Gospel of Mark had done. We also discover that some concerns which seemed vital to Mark did not appear to be so critical for Matthew.

A. The Purposes of the Gospel

Matthew intended for his version of the story of Jesus to serve two functions. The first was apologetic. By apologetic we don't mean he was trying to apologize in the sense of expressing regret or remorse for Christianity. Rather "apologetic" is being used in a special sense to indicate a defense of the Christian faith from those who are indifferent or hostile to its claims.

Matthew designed his Gospel as an apology against a hostile militant Judaism. He wanted to help his community to explain and to defend its conviction that Jesus is the Messiah in and through whom the fulfillment of God's purposes was accomplished. His Gospel was intended to be an aid in his community's debate with non-Christian Judaism.

The second purpose of Matthew's Gospel was directed more to the internal life of his community. He wanted to teach his fellow Christians. His Gospel helped Christians understand the Jewish origins of their faith, and advised them concerning the shape of that disciplined community life which was in harmony with their faith. So it instructed about the ethical implications of Christianity.

B. Some Main Ideas

1. The Law

The Mosaic law had long played a central role in the faith of Judaism. After the destruction of the Temple in Jerusalem and the end of the cultic sacrifice, the law assumed an even more fundamental importance. It was reverenced as the inspired revelation of the will of God, the heart of Judaism.

Matthew agreed with that view of the law. Jesus' teachings were not a corrective nor a substitute for the Jewish law. That law had an unconditional validity which was enduring (Matt. 5:17–20). The fault of the Jewish leaders was not in their promotion and defense of the law but, paradoxically, in their refusal to live by it (Matt. 23:1–3).

Matthew was sensitive to the problem of the application of the law to everyday life. The law had been recorded a long time ago. Many changes had taken place since. People were uncertain about how the will of God as it was made known through the Torah should be applied to their lives. The need for authoritative interpretation had long been recognized in Judaism. Matthew agreed. But he was convinced that Judaism had not provided it. The Jewish leaders simply were not capable to interpret the law, only Jesus was (Matt. 7:28–29).

The Sermon on the Mount (Matt. 5—7) did not replace the law but rather radically restated its demands in the light of the establishment of God's kingly rule ("the kingdom of heaven"). Matthew believed that Jesus understood the real nature of the law of Moses better than the rabbis. He had exposed the heart of the law when he taught that its most perfect expression was unconditioned love (Matt. 22: 36–40, cf. 5:43–48). Actually the rabbis understood the essence of Torah as love, too, as Matthew probably knew. The basic difference between Jesus and the rabbis, as Matthew understood them, was that Jesus embodied the heart of the law by the way he lived and they did not.

Just as Jesus' teachings did not replace the law but went beyond it and completed it, so Matthew did not consider Jesus as an opponent to Moses. He had not come to replace Moses but to complete what God had begun with Moses. His authority surpassed that of Moses; naturally, his teachings were a superior interpretation of the law of Moses to the teachings of the rabbis. Professor Norman Perrin has well expressed the contrast between Jesus and the rabbis as Matthew saw it. "The rabbis saw the Torah further developed by the teaching of the Mishnah and brought to completion by the Talmud. Matthew . . . sees the Torah 'fulfilled' and redefined in the teaching of Jesus (Matt. 5:17–20) and completed in the teaching function of the church (Matt. 28:16–20, especially verse 20)."[25] The disciples are charged to continue to provide authoritative interpretation (Matt. 28:20). They, and those in continuity with them (including Matthew and his colleagues) are true scribes trained for the kingdom of heaven (Matt. 13:52).

2. Rabbinical Judaism Opposed

As counterpoint to his high view of the law, Matthew developed a sharp polemic against rabbinic Judaism. Wherever he refers to "scribes and Pharisees" he has the rabbinic Judaism of his own day in mind.

Judaism was forced to recover and restore itself after its defeat by Titus at the head of the Roman legions and the catastrophe of the destruction of the Temple in Jerusalem (70 C.E.). With Jerusalem in ruins the new core around which Judaism was reorganized was a confederation of rabbinical scholars centered in Jamnia, a small town west of Jerusalem near the Mediterranean coast. The fever of nationalistic fervor had burned fiercely for many Jews during the war with Rome. Naturally they were severely disappointed at the complete defeat which the Romans had inflicted on them. The strain of survival and the stress of radical readjustments in the period which followed produced a new air of caution and wariness within Judaism. This affected Jewish attitudes toward Christianity.

Previously, Jewish indifference toward and even tolerance of the Christian movement[26] had fostered a confusion in the minds of many outsiders. Christianity appeared to be another one of the numerous sect groups within Judaism. Following the Roman conflict, however, the strain of recovery and redefinition provoked a more sharply defensive intolerance in some segments of Judaism. Matthew and his community were struggling to cope with that kind of hostile confrontation.

Matthew addressed the problem of Jewish enmity in his Gospel. He portrayed Jesus as being very sympathetic toward the Pharisees. Because the Pharisees were so devoted to the study of the law they had the potential for great faith (Matt. 23:1-3; cf. 13:52). All they had to do was understand what the law really was saying about God and how he chose to relate to his human creation. If the Pharisees could be brought to acknowledge God's saving presence in Jesus then it was likely that the rest of Israel would also respond in faith.

Jesus' public ministry was limited by and large to Israel (Matt. 15:24; cf. 10:5-7, 23). The Pharisees were that segment of Israel most concerned with understanding and correctly interpreting the real meaning of the law. They were the experts in Torah. But Jesus was the real meaning of the law. The law was exactly what Jesus had come to fulfill. The Pharisees should therefore be those most openly receptive of him. They should be his greatest supporters.

Instead they regularly resent him and are suspicious of him (Matt. 9:34; 12:24), accuse him (Matt. 9:11; 12:2; 15:1–2), try to trap him (Matt. 19:3; 22:15) and plot against him (Matt. 12:14; 21:45–46; 27:62–63). Accordingly Jesus warns his disciples to beware of them (Matt. 16:6, 11–12). The disciples should heed their teachings but not follow their example (Matt. 23:1–3). Even with their teachings caution must be exercised (Matt. 15:3–9, 12–14). True disciples are to be more righteous than they (Matt. 5:20). Their hypocrisy is obvious (Matt. 3:7–10). Terrible judgment shall be their final lot (Matt. 23).

Although the Pharisees seemed for a time to succeed (Matt. 27:1–2, 20, 41–43), God accomplished his purposes ultimately through the resurrection of Jesus in spite of their opposition. The submissive humility of Jesus in contrast to the vengeful arrogance of the Pharisees provided a model to guide Matthew's church in its struggles with hostile rabbinic Judaism.

It should be noted that Matthew's portrayal of the Pharisees was colored by several factors. He must have been influenced by the stereotyped role of opposition which the Jewish religious leaders played in the Gospel of Mark, one of his sources. Undoubtedly his description reflects a Christian prejudice nurtured by repeated experiences of hostility and rejection by Jews. Similar recent experiences resulting from his own community's contacts with rabbinic Judaism reinforced that bias. From a literary standpoint the unrelieved opposition of the Pharisees served as a foil to throw in sharp contrast the acceptance of Jesus by his disciples.

3. Doctrine of Christ

"Who do men say that the Son of man is?" (Matt. 16:13)
"You are the Christ, the Son of the living God." (Matt. 16:16)

In his account of Peter's confession of faith at Caesarea Philippi and the events following it (Matt. 16:13–28) Matthew gave the climac-

tic expression to his own conviction of who Jesus was. He is the
Messiah ("the Christ") in whom the Jewish figure of the Son of God
(cf. Matt. 3:13–17; 4:1–11; 17:1–5; etc.) and the Daniel 7:13–14
prophecy of the end-time Son of man (Matt. 9:6; 10:23; 16:27–28, etc.)
are fulfilled.

As was frequently the case in early Christianity Matthew expressed his understanding of Christ in terms of functions. What Jesus
did revealed who he was. His marvelous deeds, but above all his
authoritative teaching and his suffering martyrdom disclosed his messiahship. God confirmed his identity repeatedly, finally by raising him
from the dead. Precisely this Jesus, divinely confirmed and exalted,
continues to be present and to function authoritatively through his
church. "All authority in heaven and on earth has been given to me.
. . . I am with you always, to the close of the age" (Matt. 28:18–20).

4. The Church and Israel

The question of continuity between the Christian church and the
people of God described in the Jewish Scriptures gravely concerned
Matthew and his community. Why had historical Israel rejected
Jesus? Why was it so hostile to the church? Why was Christianity
becoming an increasingly Gentile movement?

Matthew sought to respond to these issues by redefining "Israel."
Since historical Israel willfully misunderstood its function as God's
chosen people it had lost the priority which had been implied in its
election. Its aggressive resistance to the unfolding of God's saving
purposes resulted in its condemnation. God has transferred tenancy
of the vineyard to others—the Gentiles (Matt. 21:33–43).[27] Historical
Israel is no longer religious Israel.

The church is the true Israel. It does not replace historical Israel,
but neither are they identical. Since Jesus is Messiah, the fulfillment
and completion of God's revelation in the Jewish Scriptures, those
who believe him to be Messiah are true Israelites. That can include
Jews (e.g., Peter, etc.) but does not necessarily do so. Jesus defines true
Israel. Belonging to Israel is not an accident of birth but the consequence of faith in Jesus Messiah. Those who accept him as Son of God
are the holy people of God.

Matthew did not make the mistake that he felt historical Israel had made. He did not automatically identify "Israel" with the people of the kingdom. The church is never equated with the kingly rule of God which is to come. It also will face end-time judgment (Matt. 16:25–27; 19:23–30; 20:16, 24–25). The church is Israel so long as it responds obediently to the abiding presence of its risen and exalted Lord, Jesus Messiah (Matt. 18:20; 28:20).

5. Universal Scope of the Gospel

Since historical Israel is not identical with the people of God, inclusion of believing persons other than Jews becomes possible, even necessary. The Great Commission (Matt. 28:18–20) expressed so clearly the universal validity of the work of Jesus and therefore of the gospel preached by the church. It confirms a motif occurring frequently in Matthew's Gospel.

The strong faith of the Canaanite woman gains her access to Jesus' healing power (Matt. 15:24–26). Gentiles are capable of greater faith than the Jews (Matt. 8:10). When they demonstrate superior faith they are representative of the vast geographical area from which will come all of those who, because of their faith, will have access to the table of the Patriarchs (Matt. 8:11). Their admittance to this religious table fellowship will frequently be in place of Jews who should have priority but would not believe (Matt. 8:12). Jesus fulfilled the prophecy of Isaiah which had anticipated the salvation of the Gentiles (Matt. 12:18, 21; cf. also Matt. 13:38; 22:9; 24:14; 25:32; 26:13).

If the gospel was not restricted to the Jews neither did it exclude them. The "all nations" of the Great Commission included the Jews, too (Matt. 28:19; cf. 25:32). Matthew portrayed Jesus as anticipating that some of Israel would confess him as Messiah at the second coming (Matt. 23:39). The inbreaking of the kingdom of heaven in the person of Jesus has dissolved the religious distinction between Jew and Gentile. They are one humanity. The significant distinction is no longer ethnic, but is defined in terms of discipleship which faithfully observes the teaching of Jesus (Matt. 28:19–20; cf. Matt. 13:52; 19: 16–22).

6. The End of the Ages

The Jesus traditions which Matthew included in his Gospel reflected the widespread Christian expectation of the nearness of Christ's return and of the end of the world in its present form (Matt. 4:17; 10:23; 16:28; 24:33–34). Matthew was sympathetic to that belief, since he believed that the promises in the Jewish Scriptures concerning the end-time were already being fulfilled.

He held this belief in tension with the view that the exact time when the second coming will occur is uncertain and may well be delayed for a considerable interval (Matt. 24:3–8, 26–31, 36–44; 25:1–12). There is still missionary work for the church to do (Matt. 13:36–43; 24:14; 28:16–20). Expectancy may not be abandoned or dulled (Matt. 24:27, 42–44; 25:13). But, in the interim, advice and rules for regulating the life of the community and the conduct of individual Christians are needed (Matt. 18; cf. the teachings of Jesus generally, throughout the Gospel). While not contesting a vivid end-time expectation, Matthew does redirect concern away from anxiety about when Jesus will return and toward interest in the quality of the Christian life in the interim.

IV. MATTHEW AND HIS COMMUNITY

On the basis of the features of Matthew's Gospel which we have observed above, we are able to formulate some ideas about the author and the nature of his community. Such descriptions become more graphic when other events of the first century world are recalled.

A. The Matthean Church

Matthew's community was predominantly Jewish-Christian, though it probably also contained Gentile-Christians. The church had been preaching the gospel to audiences composed of both Jews and Gentiles. The Gentiles were responding favorably to the gospel proclamation and, consequently, that part of the Christian fellowship was growing. By contrast Jewish interest and response was minimal. The Jewish attitude to the Matthean community and its message was increasingly antagonistic.

Matthew's church had been in existence for an extended period and was in an advanced stage of development both in its theology and in its corporate experiences as a Christian fellowship. It had participated in the shifting emphasis of early Christian expansion from a primary focus on Judaism to an almost exclusive focus on the Gentile world. That painful shift precipitated an identity crisis concerning the legitimacy of the appropriation by the Christian church of divine promises addressed to historical Israel and recorded in Jewish Scriptures. Matthew's church reflected residual tensions generated by that shift between the more conservative Jewish-Christian majority and the rapidly expanding Gentile-Christian component.

Relations with non-Christian Judaism were even more strident. "Matthew seems to stand on a bridge between Judaism and Christianity while the bridge is being torn asunder," observed Lamar Cope.[28] Matthew's church, along with many other Christians, was intentionally molding its self-understanding distinct from Judaism (Matt. 23: 8–12). After the disaster of the Jewish rebellion against Rome, the church totally disengaged itself from Jewish nationalism.

Post-70s Judaism entertained few illusions about Christianity as simply another Jewish sect. Too much had happened and too many flagrant violations of acceptable Jewish demeanor had occurred. Most Christians did not share their political hopes. The sense of crisis and threat which permeated the Jewish restoration movement and made it suspicious of any deviations aggravated the rupture with Christian believers.

The hostile attitude toward Christianity of evolved Pharisaic Judaism as it developed from the rabbinical schools at Jamnia is well represented by one of the rabbinic benedictions from the Birkath ha-Minim (from c. 85 C.E., around the time that Matthew wrote his Gospel):

> "For the excommunicate let there be no hope and the arrogant government do thou swiftly uproot in our days; and may the Christians and the heretics suddenly be laid low and not be inscribed with the righteous. Blessed art thou, O Lord, who humblest the arrogant."[29]

The rift between Judaism and Christianity was all but absolute.

B. The Author

The author of the first Gospel was an anonymous Jewish-Christian whose community was engaged in the Hellenistic Jewish Christian mission. He was well educated and literarily capable. He possessed considerable knowledge of rabbinic traditions and methods.

The identification of the author with Matthew, one of the Twelve is problematic. Only in the First Gospel is the tax collector whom Jesus called to be a disciple named "Matthew" (Matt. 9:9–13). Both Mark and Luke call him "Levi" (Mark 2:13–17; Luke 5:27–32). Nevertheless all three evangelists include a "Matthew" in their lists of the Twelve (Matt. 10:3; Mark 3:18; Luke 6:15; cf. Acts 1:13). Another "Matthew" joined the Twelve after the resurrection according to Luke (Acts 1:15–26).

The earliest evidence which connects the name of Matthew with a written gospel is the quotation in Eusebius (a fourth century Christian historian) from Papias, who was bishop of Hieropolis in Asia (today's Turkey) around 150 C.E. Papias was quoted as writing, "Matthew collected the logia [words of Jesus] in the Hebrew language and everybody interpreted them as he could" (H. E. III:29:16). It is unlikely that Papias was referring to the First Gospel since it was written in Greek by someone who was not an eyewitness of the ministry of Jesus but had to depend on Greek documents as sources for the Jesus traditions he used.

The composition of Matthew's Gospel must be dated after 70 C.E. since it presumes the Jewish defeat by Rome (Matt. 21:41–45; 22:7; 24:15; 27:25). If the Gospel of Mark was written around 65 C.E., time must be allowed for it to have been distributed and to be in popular use. Ignatius of Antioch, who wrote a series of letters in 110 C.E., used the earliest existing quotations from the Gospel of Matthew. It must have been written enough earlier to allow time not only for acceptance in Antioch but probably also for it to have become known by those to whom Ignatius wrote. As close an approximation of the dating of Matthew as we can now establish is 85–90 C.E.

The place of composition is also unknown, though it would have had to be in a Greek-speaking region with a large Jewish population and relatively near to Jamnia. The location suggested most often by scholars is Syria, perhaps in or near Syrian Antioch.

V. OUTLINE

I. Narrative: identity of Jesus Christ, Son of God 1:1—4:25
   A. Genealogy 1:1–17
   B. Nativity stories: birth, Wise Men, flight to Egypt 1:18—2:23
   C. Ministry of John the Baptist 3:1–12 (minor discourse: the authority of Jesus 3:7–12)
   D. Preparation for ministry 3:13—4:17 ("From that time Jesus began . . ." 4:17)
   E. Call of disciples 4:18–22
   F. Beginning of ministry in Galilee 4:23–25

II. Discourse: demands of true discipleship in end-time kingdom 5:1—7:29 (The Sermon on the Mount)
   A. Introduction and Beatitudes 5:1–12
   B. Dynamic of the kingdom: salt and light 5:13–16
   C. The law completed and fulfilled 5:17–48
   D. Worldly and kingdom piety contrasted 6:1–18
   E. The practice of genuine righteousness 6:19—7:12
   F. Warnings for obedience 7:13–27
   G. Stereotyped formula conclusion 7:28–29 ("And when Jesus finished these sayings . . ." 7:28)

III. Narrative: miraculous supernatural authority 8:1—10:4
   A. Three healings 8:1–17
   B. Sayings about discipleship 8:18–22
   C. Three miraculous works 8:23—9:8
   D. Distinguishing demands of discipleship 9:9–17
   E. Four healings stories 9:18–34
   F. Summary 9:35–36
   G. Need for disciples 9:37—10:4

IV. Discourse: charge and authority of disciples 10:5—11:1
   A. Disciples' mission to Israel 10:5–15
   B. Preparation for persecution 10:16–38
   C. Favorable reception rewarded 10:39–42
   D. Stereotyped formula conclusion 11:1 ("And when Jesus had finished instructing his twelve disciples . . ." 11:1)

V. Narrative: the Jews reject Jesus 11:2—12:50
   A. Jesus identifies himself to John the Baptist 11:2–6
   B. Jesus identifies John the Baptist 11:7–15
   C. Jews rejected both John and Jesus 11:16–19
   D. Rejecting results in judgment 11:20–24
   E. Jesus identifies himself as divine revealer 11:25–30
   F. Two controversy stories 12:1–14
   G. Rejection will be judged 12:15–37
   H. Demand for signs 12:38–45
   I. Jesus' true people 12:46–50

VI. Discourse: parables of the kingdom of heaven 13:1–58
   A. Narrative introduction 13:1–2
   B. Parable of Sower and its interpretation 13:3–23
   C. Three kingdom parables of future judgment 13:24–43
   D. Three kingdom parables on worth and selectivity 13:44–50
   E. The scribe trained for the kingdom 13:51–52
   F. Stereotyped formula conclusion 13:53 ("And when Jesus had finished these parables . . ." 13:53)
   G. Jesus' own neighbors reject him 13:54–58

VII. Narrative: disciples accept Jesus 14:1—17:27
   A. Identity of Jesus: Herod killed John the Baptist 14:1–12
   B. Feeding of 5000 14:13–21
   C. Walking on the water and faith 14:22–36
   D. Controversy over cultic uncleanness 15:1–20
   E. Jesus has compassion on Gentiles 15:21–39
   F. Pharisaic adversaries 16:1–12
   G. Peter's confession 16:13–20
   H. Jesus' prediction of suffering and return 16:21–28 ("From that time Jesus began . . ." 16:21)
   I. Identity of Jesus: transfiguration 17:1–8
   J. John the Baptist is Elijah 17:9–13
   K. Faith makes whole: healing of epileptic 17:14–20
   L. Jesus' second prediction of suffering 17:22–23
   M. The Temple tax 17:24–27

VIII. Discourse: charge and authority of the church 18:1—19:2
   A. Pastoral care of new converts 18:1–14
   B. Discipline of new converts 18:15–35
   C. Stereotyped formula conclusion 19:1–2 ("Now when Jesus had finished these sayings . . ." 19:1)

IX. Narrative: authority and invitation 19:3—22:46
   A. Divorce and celibacy 19:3–12
   B. Blessing of children 19:13–15
   C. The rich young man 19:16–26
   D. Parable of the Laborers 20:1–16
   E. Jesus' third prediction of suffering 20:17–28
   F. Two blind men healed 20:29–34
   G. Triumphal entry 21:1–11
   H. Cleansing of Temple 21:12–17
   I. Cursing of the fig tree 21:18–22
   J. Controversies with scribes, Pharisees, Sadducees 21:23—22:46

X. Discourse: end-time judgment on false discipleship 23:1—26:2
   A. The Pharisees' bad example 23:1–12
   B. Seven woes of judgment against the scribes and Pharisees 23:13–36
   C. Lament over Jerusalem 23:37–39
   D. Signs of the end of time 24:1–36
   E. Exhortations to be ready 24:37–51
   F. Three end-of-time stories 25:1–46
   G. Stereotyped formula conclusion 26:1–2 ("When Jesus had finished all these sayings . . ." 26:1)

XI. Narrative: Jesus as suffering and vindicated Messiah 26:3—28:20
   A. Plot and preparation for Jesus' death 26:3–16
   B. The Last Supper 26:17–29
   C. Prediction of disciples' dereliction 26:30–35
   D. Gethsemane 26:36–46
   E. Betrayal, arrest, and trial before Caiaphas 26:47–68
   F. Peter's denial 26:69–75
   G. Judas' fate; trial before Pilate 27:1–26
   H. The crucifixion 27:27–56
   I. The burial 27:57–66
   J. The women and the resurrected Jesus 28:1–10
   K. The false report of the guard 28:11–15
   L. Appearance to the disciples 28:16–20 (minor discourse: Jesus identifies the authority of the church 28:18–20)

CHAPTER FOUR
Why Expand a Gospel?
The Gospel of Luke

The author of the Gospel of Luke has been identified traditionally as a missionary colleague of the Apostle Paul. As will be seen below this identification causes difficulties today. Nevertheless whoever wrote the Third Gospel made the largest contribution to the composition of the New Testament of any of its authors. When this Gospel is joined by its companion volume, the Acts of the Apostles, they together make up about twenty-seven percent or a little better than one-fourth of the New Testament. That is more than the entire Pauline corpus.[1]

This chapter will describe some literary features of the Gospel, examine Luke's use of his sources, consider the theological interests and literary purposes that were important to Luke, review what can be known about the author and outline the contents of the Gospel.

I. SOME LITERARY CONSIDERATIONS

A. *Luke's Second Volume*

The most distinctive feature of Luke's writing, differentiating him from the other Gospel composers, was the sequel which he wrote to accompany his Gospel: the Acts of the Apostles.[2] None besides Luke sought to extend the narrative beyond the time of Jesus.

But aren't the Third Gospel and the book of Acts simply two works by the same author (as Shakespeare wrote *Hamlet* and *Twelfth Night*)? To conceive of the two volumes as such distorts and misleads. Rather they are two parts of a single literary work. Luke composed them as a unity, intending that they be read together. The prefaces to the two volumes make this plain (Luke 1:-1–4; Acts 1:1–5). His intent has been obscured by the order of the New Testament canon (the list of books in the New Testament). The Gospel of John intrudes between the two parts of the Lukan work. Until this is called to their attention many readers overlook the continuity Luke sustained between the contents of the two volumes.

Luke intended to describe how the salvation of God had been accomplished and was being announced.

> The first volume tells how the salvation promised to Israel was realized through the birth, life, passion, and resurrection of Jesus of Nazareth. The second volume tells how appointed witnesses proclaimed this salvation in Jerusalem, Samaria, and even wider circles, so that the word of God grew and even Gentiles became participants in that salvation.[3]

One major effect that resulted from Luke's extension of his narrative of Jesus with a companion narrative of the spread of the gospel by the church was the heightening of the historical perspective of the first volume. As he drew attention to God's continuing activity in and through the apostolic church (and by implied extension, in and through his own church), Luke intensified the impression that the life of Jesus—his ministry, death, and resurrection—was an event that belonged to a past epoch in human history which was unique.

By way of comparison we might say that Mark told the story of Jesus to clarify and convict his hearers concerning the present claims of the exalted Lord for their faithful, informed allegiance. Matthew historicized the Jesus traditions but emphasized their present relevance through his use of the "promise-fulfillment" pattern. Luke conceived of the interval of Jesus' life as a unique period of time distinct from the time of the church.[4]

B. Structure

Luke adopted the structure of the Gospel of Mark as the basic pattern for his own Gospel. His narrative of the life of Jesus also contains, as did Mark's Gospel, an early period of ministry in Galilee and a later period in Jerusalem, where Jesus was executed and resurrected.

Luke added to the beginning of the story structure which he found in Mark the John the Baptist infancy stories (chapter 1), the infancy and nativity narratives of Jesus, and his genealogy (chapters 2 and 3). He also expanded Mark's conclusion to include post-resurrection appearance traditions (Luke 24:13–53).

The most obvious internal alteration to Mark's structure appears with the journey account. In Mark the transition journey which takes Jesus from the region of Galilee to Jerusalem is described in a little over one chapter (Mark 10:1—11:10). Luke stretched his version of that journey narrative over almost ten chapters (Luke 9:51—19:40).

This narrative expansion enabled Luke to include a great amount of additional teaching material that is not in Mark. Jesus is portrayed as addressing these teachings mostly to his disciples. Since the journey was begun soon after the first prediction by Jesus of his own martyrdom (Luke 9:44) the sign of the cross looms over it all.

> The Lord who is on his way to suffer according to the will of God is equipping his disciples for carrying on his preaching after his death (Luke 9:60; 10:3, 16; 17:22–25).[5]

The effect is much the same as what Mark had accomplished by narratively connecting the individual oral traditions of Jesus to the passion narrative. Crucifixion and resurrection become the interpretive key to full, correct understanding of these teachings of Jesus.

A prominent and significant structural feature of Luke's writings is the striking parallelism of components in the third Gospel and in Acts. Comparison between the two reveals these correspondences:

1) Preface with dedication to Theophilus (Luke 1:1–4; Acts 1:1–5)
2) Filled with the Holy Spirit (Luke 3:21–22; Acts 2:1–4)
3) Forty day period of preparation before ministry (Luke 4:2; Acts 1:3)

4) Ministry inaugurated with sermon thematically anticipating rejection which will occur (Luke 4:16–30; Acts 2:14–40)
5) Authoritative teaching and wondrous deeds evoke conflict, unbelief, and rejection (Luke 4:31—8:56; Acts 3:1—12:17)
6) Mission to the Gentiles prominent (Luke 10:1–12; Acts 13 —19:20)
7) Journey to Jerusalem and martyrdom (Luke 9:51—23:49; Acts 19:21—21:17)

In addition there are striking parallels in the events which take place while both Jesus and Paul are in Jerusalem, and in the details of the accounts of their trials. The above list is only partial,[6] yet the correspondences are remarkable.

These parallels in the narrative events of Luke and Acts declare Jesus to be the model whom the church must emulate if it is to be faithful to its mission. His acts, words, and experiences provide the pattern for the acts and teachings of the church. Furthermore the fidelity of the apostolic community to that pattern guarantees to all who are in continuity with them accurate access to the true Jesus tradition.[7]

II. USE OF SOURCES

A. Stylistic Observations

Luke wrote fine Greek. Of all of the authors of the New Testament literature only the author of the Epistle to the Hebrews was in his class as a literary artist and craftsman. The preface to Luke's Gospel contains the best Greek in the entire New Testament.

That is not to suggest that Luke revived the polished style of composition characteristic of the authors of the Greek classical period such as Homer or Sophocles. Rather Luke wrote in the popular, non-literary Greek in common use in the first century, C.E. But he had a flair for style and a well-developed sense of rhetorical sentence structure. He had mastered the rules of grammar and syntax and was proficient in the art of Greek composition.

A fascinating aspect of Luke's style was his ability to adopt a Septuagintal (scriptural) tone when it suited his purposes. In effect he was consciously casting his composition into "Bible language."

We often do the same. When one friend complains to another about the harshness of a low grade received in a course and the other friend replies, "Thou shalt not be bitter," the second friend has adopted the mode of Bible language. The reply is formulated to conform to the style of the Ten Commandments of Exodus 20 and even employs the archaic forms of the Elizabethan English used in the King James Version of the Bible. It's Bible language.

Luke did something similar, though in a much more sophisticated way than the above analogy suggests. Of course his "Bible" wasn't the King James Version but the Greek translation of the Jewish Scriptures, the Septuagint. The sections where Luke concentrated Hebraisms (phrases and expressions which are typical of Greek corrupted by Hebrew) were the birth and infancy sections of his Gospel and the first half of Acts. The style of imitating Bible language induces the hearer to make associations between what is being recounted in Bible language and traditions already in Scriptures. It also subtly claims for itself some of the persuasiveness of biblical authority.

Another observation about Luke's style relates to the use he made of his sources. We have seen that Matthew characteristically reduced the material in his sources to isolated traditions and individual sayings. Then he reorganized them into collections (miracle collections, parable collections, etc.) and speeches (the Sermon on the Mount, the church discipline discourse, etc.).

Luke incorporated the material from his sources differently from Matthew's way. Typically, Luke included relatively large portions of material first from one source, then from another. So, for instance, most of what he used from Mark appears in three large blocks: Luke 3:1—6:19; 8:4—9:50; 18:15—24:11, and from Q in two: Luke 6:20—8:3 and 9:51—18:14.

Luke employed a large variety of literary devices to join together the materials he had gathered from his sources. Predictions which anticipated, summaries which reviewed, and cross-references which connected several traditions together all contributed to integrate the separate parts into a whole. Luke was much more thorough in shaping his sources into a literary unity than was either Mark or Matthew.

B. Mark as a Source

According to the two-source hypothesis we considered earlier, Luke had a copy of the Gospel of Mark before him. He used it as a major source of material when he composed his own Gospel. It seems reasonable to assume, as we assumed with Matthew,[8] that Luke's community was also familiar with Mark's Gospel. If that is correct it suggests that they probably would have made frequent and repeated use of Mark in preaching the gospel to non-Christians, in teaching, and in the worship of their community. They would likely be aware therefore of many of the changes Luke made to Mark's narrative. They would also be alert for any new ideas which Luke invested in his revision of Mark.

Luke incorporated most of Mark—almost seventy percent—into his Gospel. That is less, however, than Matthew who used around ninety percent of Mark. In these Markan sections Luke preserved Mark's narrative sequence with exceptional exactness. However, he did insert some non-Markan traditions.

Omitted from Luke's Gospel was the material in Mark 6:45—8:27. Some scholars think that Luke's copy of Mark lacked that section. Others believe Luke purposely left it out because it contradicted his understanding of the geography of Jesus' ministry. No really satisfactory explanation for this omission has been given.[9]

Although Luke adopted Mark's outline as the basic framework for his own Gospel he expanded Mark considerably. He added extensive birth and infancy stories to the beginning, and post-resurrection appearance accounts to the end. In addition to the brief insertions he made into the blocks of Markan material he included two extensive sections of non-Markan traditions, Luke 6:20—8:3 and 9:51—18:14. These are sometimes called the small interpolation and the great interpolation. You will recognize that the great interpolation accounts for most of Luke's expanded travel narrative (Luke 9:51—19:40).

One surprising place where Luke diverged from Mark's narrative was with his relating of the Passion narrative, the account of the events in Jerusalem culminating in Jesus' crucifixion. Although some scholars have felt that the difference occurred because Luke's copy of the Gospel of Mark lacked that portion of the story of Jesus the evidence does not demand such a conjecture.

Luke may have had another version of the Passion story from one of his other sources that he preferred to Mark's version. Equally possible is the suggestion that he used Mark's Passion narrative but thoroughly reworked it by changing the sequence of some events and adding additional features from other sources. Certainly we can observe the extensive changes he made to Mark's version elsewhere. In any event, since the traditions about Jesus' crucifixion and resurrection would be the most precious recollections of the community, it seems likely that Luke diverged from Mark at this point to make his account conform more closely to the version his community preferred. Remember that they probably were familiar with Mark's rendition also and so were already aware of different versions.

As we noted above, Luke wrote exceptionally fine Greek, especially when he was not imitating "Bible language" by accommodating his writing style to the style of the Greek version of the Jewish Scriptures. Since Mark's Greek was rather primitive we are not surprised to discover that Luke frequently improved Mark's style. He simplified constructions, removed unnecessary repetitions, corrected grammar, and replaced colloquialisms.

Of course Matthew improved Mark's language when he rewrote his Gospel also, but Luke revised Mark much more drastically. Curiously, Luke showed considerable reserve in improving the language of the sayings of Jesus in Mark. The words of Jesus are hardly altered at all. That reticence probably reflects the great reverence in which Luke held Jesus' sayings.

Mark had depended heavily on simple conjunctions and adverbs such as "and," "again," "and then," to connect his oral traditions materials into a narrative sequence. "Immediately" was one of his favorites. Luke reduced drastically the number of vague, adverbial connectives. In their place he provided more specific and concrete connecting links. Compare, for example, Mark's *"And* a leper came to him beseeching . . ." (Mark 1:40, italics added) with *"While he was in one of the cities,* there came a man full of leprosy . . ." (Luke 5:12, italics added). Or compare "The Spirit *immediately* drove him out into the wilderness . . ." (Mark 1:12, italics added) with *"And Jesus, full of the Holy Spirit, returned from the Jordan,* and was led by the Spirit . . ." (Luke 4:1, italics added). Luke's revision provided a smoother and more lively narrative flow.

Luke improved Mark's grammatical style of expression. He was more severe than even Matthew on Mark's fondness for the historical present.[10] Whereas Matthew retained 21 instances of the 151 times Mark used that tense, in Luke only 1 survived. Frequently Luke corrected Mark's faulty use of the imperfect tense to the more literarily accurate aorist tense.[11] Luke often favored substituting compound verbs for the simple verbs Mark usually employed.

Mark used colloquial words and phrases which Luke altered into more elegant Greek. Loan-words, words taken over into Greek from other languages, were changed by Luke into proper Greek expressions. Mark's "Rabbi" (Mark 9:5; 10:51) becomes "Master" (Luke 9:33) or "Lord" (Luke 18:41). "Simon the Cananaean" is changed to "Simon the Zealot" (Mark 3:18; Luke 6:15). The Latin term "centurion" which had been adopted into popular Greek was replaced by Luke with the proper Greek equivalent for the Latin term (Mark 15:39; Luke 23:47). (Our English versions render Luke's expression "centurion" also, because that Latin word has now become a part of our English vocabulary as it had then of Mark's Greek.) Luke simply omitted some Hebrew words that he found in Mark. "Boanerges," "Iscariot," "abba," "hosanna" all are lacking. "Amen" usually is dropped, or, occasionally, changed to "truly."

There is one feature of Luke's linguistic style which, because of scholarly overstatement, has caused confusion. Scholars often have claimed that the large amount of technical medical vocabulary in Luke-Acts strongly supports the thesis that the author was a physician. Actually medicine in the first century, C.E., was still an infant science. Most of its vocabulary was shared by those educated to other occupations. All that Luke's elaborate vocabulary establishes is that he was well educated, not that he was, necessarily, a doctor.[12] Of course, it does not disprove that assumption either.

Often Luke abbreviated Mark's version. By eliminating redundancies and unessential details he tightened many narrative accounts. For instance Luke told about the miraculous feeding of the five thousand more effectively in eight verses (Luke 9:10–17) than did Mark in fifteen (Mark 6:30–44). Comparison of the two accounts shows the details Luke left out to make the account more compact. He completely omitted the companion tradition in Mark of the miraculous feeding of the four thousand (Mark 8:1–10), apparently because he found it redundant. Another brief example of the way Luke condensed portions of Mark is the difference in their two versions of the parable of the sower (Mark 4:1–9; Luke 8:4–8).

Luke's great reverence for Jesus and his disciples led him to omit certain features found in Mark that he considered offensive. References to Jesus reacting in a humanly emotional way were reduced. Jesus healed the leper in both Mark and Luke but not out of *pity* in Luke (cf. Mark 1:41 and Luke 5:13). Jesus' grief and anger at Pharisaic criticism (cf. Mark 3:5; Luke 6:10) as well as his love for a hesitant disciple (cf. Mark 10:21; Luke 18:22) apparently implied too mortal a person for Luke's view of Christ. Even on the cross, Jesus' cry of dereliction ("My God, my God, why hast thou forsaken me?" Mark 15:34) was changed by Luke to the more tranquil expression "Father, into thy hands I commit my spirit" (Luke 23:46).

Luke also improved Mark's portrayal of the disciples. He left out, "they all forsook him and fled," the phrase with which Mark explicitly described the disciples' desertion of Jesus (Mark 14:50; cf. Luke 22:53). In Mark's version of the Gethsemane tradition Jesus found the disciples sleeping three times (Mark 14:37, 40, 41). Luke recognized that this was a very negative criticism against the disciples (it paralleled Peter's three-fold denial). He reduced the times they were caught asleep to one and added, by way of excuse, that they slept "for sorrow" (Luke 22:45).

C. "Q"

The Gospel of Mark was not the only source which Luke had in common with Matthew. Both Matthew and Luke also drew on Q for additional Jesus traditions to those they found in Mark. It might be helpful at this point to review the discussion of the nature of Q by referring to pp. 85ff. and to the list of contents of Q on pp. 87ff. above.

Since Luke incorporated material from the Gospel of Mark in

large blocks we would expect him to do something similar with Q. Most of the material Luke took from Q is concentrated in two large sections, Luke 6:20—8:3 and 9:51—18:14. The latter section is, of course, the bulk of Luke's expanded version of the journey of Jesus from Galilee to Jerusalem.

When scholars compare the Q traditions in Matthew and Luke they usually assume that the order of the material in Luke conforms more nearly to that of Q than does Matthew's order. Since Luke preserved the order of Mark's Gospel more carefully than Matthew it is a likely presumption that he did the same with Q.

We have no way to test the extent to which Luke reworked the language and style of the Q material he borrowed. Grammatical corrections, linguistic refinement, and stylistic improvement may only be suspected. On the analogy of the manner in which he revised Mark, however, we may suppose that he dealt similarly with the traditions he took from Q.

D. "L"

The Gospel of Luke is much longer than the sum of the combined materials which Luke adopted from Mark and from Q. Over one-third of the Third Gospel relates traditions which are in Luke alone. Neither Matthew nor Mark tell of the "shepherds out in the field, keeping watch over their flock by night" (Luke 2:8–20), a scene so evocative of the Christmas celebration. Nor do the first two Gospels know of the Parable of the Prodigal Son (Luke 15:11–32). Nor do they relate the story of the resurrected Christ walking with two discouraged disciples along the road to Emmaus, who did not recognize their traveling companion until the moment when he broke bread with them (Luke 24:13–35).

The nativity stories and the infancy traditions with which Luke began his Gospel (Luke 1 and 2) are peculiar to him. So also is his genealogy of Jesus (Luke 3:23–38). (Matthew also recorded a genealogy of Jesus but it differs from Luke's—compare Matt. 1:1–17). As we have already seen[13] the divergencies from Mark's account of Jesus' trial and crucifixion in Luke's version probably resulted from the influence of a different passion tradition which the Lukan community preferred to Mark's version.

The special material found in the main body of Luke's Gospel greatly enriches our knowledge of ancient Jesus traditions treasured by the early church. They include five otherwise unknown miracle stories:

> Miraculous catch of fish (Luke 5:1–11)
> Resuscitation of the widow of Nain's son (Luke 7:11–17)
> Healing of the infirm woman (Luke 13:10–17)
> Healing of the man with dropsy (Luke 14:1–6)
> Healing of the ten lepers (Luke 17:11–19).

Luke adds fourteen additional parables and similitudes to the collection Mark and Matthew had preserved for the church:

> The two debtors (Luke 7:40–43)
> The good Samaritan (Luke 10:29–37)
> The friend at midnight (Luke 11:5–8)
> The rich fool (Luke 12:13–21)
> The barren fig tree (Luke 13:6–9)
> On building a tower (Luke 14:28–30)
> On going to war (Luke 14:31–32)
> The lost coin (Luke 15:8–10)
> The prodigal son (Luke 15:11–32)
> The unjust steward (Luke 16:1–12)
> The rich man and Lazarus (Luke 16:19–31)
> The servant's duties (Luke 17:7–10)
> The unjust judge (Luke 18:1–8)
> The Pharisee and the publican (Luke 18:9–14).

When we add the story of the Samaritan villages which rejected Jesus (Luke 9:51–56) and the story of Zacchaeus (Luke 19:1–10) we cannot help but marvel at the rich quality of special traditions which Luke has made available to us.[14]

Scholars frequently refer to all of the special traditions which are found only in the Gospel of Luke with the symbol "L." As was the case with "M" (Matthew's special traditions) and with "Q" (traditions common to both Matthew and Luke) we cannot be certain that "L" was only one document. Probably it was not. It is very doubtful that Luke derived all of his special traditions from just one additional written source. Rather he may have gathered some of the "L" material from several other documents. Very likely much of it was borrowed by him from the common fund of oral traditions. The designation "L" is simply a symbol of convenience to indicate traditions unique to the Third Gospel.

We may now recall the chart of the interrelationship of the Synoptic Gospels begun on p. 85. It can be completed for the Gospel of Luke as follows:

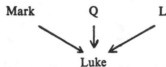

By combining this diagram with the one drawn earlier for the Gospel of Matthew (p. 98), the literary relationship of the Synoptic Gospels, (the first three Gospels in the New Testament), may be represented thus:

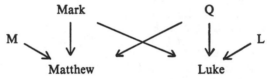

III. WHY LUKE WROTE HIS GOSPEL

Clearly Luke had to have some specific reasons for going to the trouble of writing his two-volume work. As with the Gospel of Matthew, the changes which Luke made as he revised Mark's Gospel provide helpful clues for us as we try to discern what his reasons were.

Unlike either Matthew or Mark, Luke announced right at the beginning of his Gospel what he was intending to do. "Many have undertaken to compile a narrative of the things which have been accomplished among us . . . it seemed good to me . . . to write an orderly account . . . that you may know the truth" (Luke 1:1–4). Luke knew of other accounts already written but, much as he admired them and had learned from them, he considered them to be inadequate. That is implied by his resolve "to write an orderly account" even though many had already "undertaken to compile a narrative." He wanted to do better than they had.

Luke was determined to write a better Gospel than any he knew. He intended for his literary composition to replace those other accounts rather than to be used along with them. It is an interesting irony that later the church clustered Luke's Gospel together with several others as complements to each other. At least one in that group of Gospels was one that Luke had intended to supercede—the Gospel of Mark.

In what ways did he try to improve on what had already been done?

A. Luke's Purposes

1. Accuracy

Luke sought to make his Gospel more accurate. He considered himself to be competent to compose "a narrative of the things which have been accomplished among us . . . having followed all things closely for some time past, to write an orderly account" (Luke 1:1, 3). Luke was a first century Christian historian. He wanted to write a history of the life of Jesus, the Savior. In his second volume, Acts, he wrote a history of how the salvation God realized in Jesus was preached by his church in expanding waves after the resurrection.

Luke did the best he could to write accurate history. Yet by the criteria of modern historical study he fell short of his intent. Before we judge his achievement too harshly, however, there are a couple of moderating observations which are very important for us to consider.

Luke assumed his sources were historical records which contained accurate information. They were at least only one stage removed from the dependable testimony of those who had been present and observed the events which the traditions described. They had been "delivered to us by those who from the beginning were eyewitnesses and ministers of the word" (Luke 1:2).

Unfortunately the confidence Luke invested in his sources was excessive. Since Luke used large portions of Mark and adopted the narrative sequence of that Gospel as the framework for his own he apparently regarded Mark as an accurate historical record. The major way he sought to improve Mark was not to correct him (with the possible exception of the Passion narrative). He tried to complete

Mark's account by enriching it with important Jesus traditions which Mark lacked. We now are quite certain, however, that Mark was not an eyewitness, himself, nor was he trying to write a history of Jesus. Many of his geographical designations and much of the chronological sequence of events in his narrative were governed by theological and literary interests.[15] Similar historical inaccuracies were likely present in the other sources upon which Luke depended.

The second excusing observation is the difference between what is meant by "history" today and what it meant in the first century. Since the Enlightenment (a philosophical movement of the seventeenth and eighteenth centuries which stressed the power of human reason), historical inquiry has developed a stringent methodology which controls certainty about factual accuracy. It is wrong to think historians of the first century weren't concerned for accurate information. They were. But that was not the chief goal of history. History was a branch of rhetoric whose usefulness lay in its interpretation of past occurrences for the illumination they could provide to enrich the meaning of the present and the future. Facts about the past, in and of themselves, were not important. What those facts signified were. If the meaning discerned in events could be made more vivid by adding details to the accounts the historian had at his disposal, then it was not only acceptable, it was his duty as a historian to provide them.

That was the kind of historian Luke was. He wrote the history of Jesus and of the early church not just to report what had occurred. The history of Jesus and the church was significant because it was a continuation of the biblical history recorded in the Jewish Scriptures, and extended into the present of Luke and his community. Luke, the historian, was also Luke, the Christian. His account was at the service of his faith.

2. Persuasiveness

Luke hoped his Gospel would be more persuasive than the other narratives which had been composed before his. He hoped to call forth from his hearers confident conviction in the content of Christian preaching by accumulating and attractively presenting a narrative of the Jesus traditions.

He wishes to recover and reformulate the roots of Christian faith so
that the certainty and continuity of Christian faith from the beginning
up to the present can be established: from Israel through Jesus to the
church.[16]

Luke also sought to make his Gospel more current for his hearers.
He wanted to provide his Christian community with resources and
counsel which addressed the critical issues with which they were
struggling. It wasn't that Mark was wrong. It was just that he had
written his Gospel to meet the needs of his community. Those concerns and the concerns of Luke's community did not exactly correspond. Luke made the Jesus traditions more relevant to the situation
of his own community.

It is true that in the preface Luke addressed his Gospel to Theophilus (Luke 1:3), an unknown Roman official who had already been
instructed in the Christian faith. But Theophilus was not the sole
intended reader. Luke was addressing himself primarily to his Christian community. He intended that they not just have more accurate
knowledge about Christianity. Even more, he was eager for them "to
know the truth concerning the things of which [they] have been
informed" (Luke 1:4). As the result of their hearing the contents of
his two-volume work they "should be strengthened in their faith,
praise God for the salvation sent to them, and take courage, so that
the number of believers might continue to increase."[17]

3. Apologetic

Luke molded his literature to serve as an apologia, a defense of
Christianity, trained in two directions. In the event that portions of
his audience were indifferent to the full claims of Christianity he
hoped to commend it to their acceptance. He explained the basis of
the Christian faith and promoted the truth of its claims.

That does not mean that Luke anticipated that pagans would read
his writing simply out of curiosity. Rather he was looking beyond the
internal concerns of his community to its involvement in Christian
missionary preaching and teaching. He wanted his work to be a
helpful resource to the other Christians as they preached Christianity.

The name of Luke's patron, Theophilus (literally "God-lover"), calls to mind a special segment of people in first century Greek society. They were Gentiles who were attracted to the Jewish religion. They associated themselves with the synagogue, participated in its worship and festivals, and adopted many Jewish customs and practices. But without becoming full converts to Judaism. The Jews called them "devout ones," "God-fearers," "God-lovers." Luke may have had that group in mind also. They were a group likely to be receptive to the gospel since they were acquainted already with Jewish traditions about the Messiah.

The second direction in which Luke pointed his apologetic was toward Imperial Rome. The term with which he addressed Theophilus, "most excellent," was a term commonly used to address high government officials (cf. Acts 23:26; 24:2; 26:25). Possibly, Luke was concerned to correct any misunderstandings Theophilus had about the nature and intent of the Christian movement. Further, Luke was the only New Testament author to name Roman emperors in his writings (Luke 2:1; 3:1; cf. also Acts 11:28; 18:2). He seems to have been sensitive to that segment of the society in which his community lived.

Luke made a considerable effort to exonerate the Roman Empire from any direct guilt for the execution of Jesus (Luke 23:4, 7, 13–16, 22, 47) and for the persecution of the Christian church (a frequent motif in Acts). He was concerned to portray Christianity as an apolitical movement. It was not a subversive sect of revolutionaries intent on overthrowing Imperial Rome. Luke even hinted that since God was at work in the Christian church, governmental authority was incapable ultimately of suppressing the Christian faith.

B. Some Main Ideas

1. Doctrine of Christ

Luke's understanding of the person and work of Jesus was molded by his knowledge of the Jewish Scripture traditions about the expected Messiah. Jesus is the anointed one sent by God. All three Synoptic authors recorded the tradition of Jesus' teaching in the synagogue at Nazareth (Matt. 13:54–58; Mark 6:1–6; Luke 4:16–30). But only Luke included the text from Jewish Scriptures which Jesus read. It was from the prophet Isaiah:

"The Spirit of the Lord is upon me,
because he has anointed me to preach good news to the poor.
He has sent me to proclaim release to the captives
and recovering of sight to the blind,
to set at liberty those who are oppressed,
to proclaim the acceptable year of the Lord."

(Luke 4:18–19; from Isaiah 61:1–2; 58:6)

Then, in Luke's version, Jesus explicitly applied the lection to himself. "Today this scripture has been fulfilled in your hearing" (Luke 4:21).

The importance of this passage for Luke's view of Christ is indicated by the prominence he gives it in his narrative. The preaching in Nazareth is the first public act of ministry which Jesus did after he had been anointed with the Spirit of God at his baptism. It follows immediately after the account of his temptation in the wilderness. This is one of the few places where Luke diverged from the order of events Mark followed in his Gospel. Mark's version of the tradition of Jesus' preaching in the synagogue is briefer, less specific, and appears only after Jesus has been engaged in ministry for some time (Mark 6:1–6). The contrast of treatment and location between Mark and Luke alerts us to the exceptional significance this tradition bore for Luke's understanding of Jesus.

If Jesus was the Messiah toward which the Jewish Scriptures pointed why wasn't he recognized and acclaimed as such during his life? That was a problem with which the early church continually struggled. In Luke's Gospel, even the disciples were able to recognize that Jesus was the promised Messiah of the Jewish Scriptures only after the resurrection when the risen Christ opened their minds to finally comprehend who he was (Luke 24:26–27, 44–48). Professor Dahl rightly observed, "Luke has retained and even sharpened the idea of the 'messianic secret' which is otherwise much more prominent in Mark."[18]

In one particular instance, Luke takes a markedly different position from the other Gospel writers. The crucifixion of Jesus is not a saving act. It is not a ransom for human sin. It is a murder perpetrated by the Jews. The saving event was the life and work of Jesus, the Messiah of God. God confirmed Jesus' messianic identity and vindicated him over his enemies with the resurrection. Jesus, the building stone rejected by the Jewish leaders, was used by God. (The image is from Psalm 118:22, a favorite text of Luke's.) The person of Jesus is unique. His life and work, however, is a model by which the church is to be guided. In Jesus the church sees how it must live now that it also is filled with the Spirit of God.

2. Holy Spirit

Luke emphasized the work of the Holy Spirit in his Gospel. The nativity and infancy stories which precede Jesus' public ministry contain numerous references to the Holy Spirit (Luke 1:15, 35, 41, 67, 80; 2:25–27). Just after the baptism of Jesus the Holy Spirit descended upon him (Luke 3:21–22) and filled him (Luke 4:1). This same Spirit led him into the wilderness to undergo the ordeal of the temptation (Luke 4:1–13). It caused him to return to Galilee to begin his public ministry (Luke 4:14–15). As we have seen, the inaugural event of that ministry was his appearance in the synagogue at Nazareth. There he identified himself as the One anointed with the Spirit of the Lord whom the prophet, Isaiah, had described (Luke 4:16–21).

Luke seems to have envisioned Jesus as anointed with the Holy Spirit in a special way. During the narration of his public ministry he is the only one Luke described as filled with the Holy Spirit. After his baptism Jesus is the sole bearer of the Spirit. John the Baptist anticipated that Jesus would communicate the Holy Spirit to his followers (Luke 3:16), an anticipation that Jesus himself confirmed (Acts 1:5, 8), and that happened at Pentecost (Acts 2:1–4). The rest of the book of Acts is filled with references to the activity of the Holy Spirit among the first Christians. But there is an important distinction between the way the Holy Spirit filled Jesus and the way the disciples were filled. Although Jesus was led by the Spirit he had control over the Spirit. The disciples and other early Christians were controlled by the Spirit.

The Holy Spirit was an important factor providing continuity within Luke's understanding of holy history (that is, history by means of which God accomplishes his saving purposes). The leaders of Israel, particularly the prophets and the other authors of Jewish Scripture were inspired by the Holy Spirit to testify to the coming of the Savior Messiah. It was by means of the Holy Spirit that Jesus, that expected Messiah, was incarnate, taught, and did miraculous works.

The early disciples and later Christians were able by the empowering of the Holy Spirit to testify persuasively and do miraculous deeds. The Holy Spirit guided the church in its missionary expansion.

3. Delay of Jesus' Return

During the first stages of the formation of the Christian community the expectation that Jesus would return right away was very common. But as months became years and even decades the anticipation that he would return soon was shaken. After all, it is very difficult breathlessly to await an event for an extended period of time.

Luke modified the current Christian expectation of the return of Christ. He relaxed the note of urgent immediacy. *When* Jesus will come again is less important than the conviction that he *is coming* again. The moment of his return has receded into the indefinite future. Breathless expectation has been muffled.[19]

Luke's modifications of the emphasis on an early return of Jesus served two purposes. First, it helped him to cope with the crisis which disappointed expectations fostered. Since the expectation of an immediate return of Jesus was so prominent in early Christianity the truth of the whole gospel message was jeopardized when it did not occur. If Christ's return hadn't occurred perhaps the rest of the Christian faith was also wrong. By muting the emphasis on the nearness of the second coming of Jesus Luke helped avert that challenge to the truth of the gospel.

Second, the extension of the interim period between the earthly ministry of Jesus and his second coming invited theological reflection. If the return of Jesus was not to be looked for right away, the time prior to his return possibly was more significant than just a lull in salvation history. Luke described it as the time of the church's work and witness in the world. It was an interval in which the spirit empowered agents of God, the church, was accomplishing a task which was an integral part of God's saving purpose. Luke was the first of the Gospel writers to develop an extensive theology of the church.

4. Salvation History

Luke was a historian. He was also a Christian. In the first century, C.E., history was considered important for the meaning it was able to discover in human events. The meaning that interested Luke most was what history disclosed about God's plan to save and restore his creation. That was a theological perspective of history which Luke found affirmed in Judaism's understanding of its history as holy history. The Jewish Scriptures amply testified to that view.[20]

Human history, rightly understood, reveals God at work to save his creation. This is so because God has chosen to make himself known through human events and historical persons. Salvation history is not identical with secular history. It is possible to know the data of history—people, places, dates, events—and still be ignorant of (or even hostile to) God's design of redemption. But secular history provides the context into which God inserts his saving presence. In that context the divine plan for salvation unfolds.

That is why Luke was so interested in including specific references to well-known persons and events in his two-volume narrative (Luke 1:5; 2:1–2; 3:1–2; cf. also Acts 11:28; 12:20–23; 18:12, etc.). He wanted to integrate the story of Jesus' life and the history of the church into a comprehensive understanding of God's redemptive history unfolding in secular history.

Luke conceived of salvation history as divided into three major epochs: the period of Israel, the period of Jesus, the period of the church.[21] Of course Luke's community was living in the third period, the period of the church.

The period of Israel was in the remote past. It stretched all the way back to creation (note that Luke's genealogy of Jesus goes back to Adam whereas the earliest figure in Matthew's genealogy is Abraham —Luke 3:23–38, compare Matt. 1:2–16). This was the period of the law and the prophets. It was the time of the revelation of God's intent to save his creation, the time of anticipation and promise. John the Baptist belonged to this period (Luke 16:16). His function was that of the prophet who prepared the way for the Messiah (Luke 1:76–77). It was in that sense that he was "filled with the Holy Spirit" (Luke 1:15b–17). But when the period of Jesus was ready to begin John the Baptist receded into the background (Luke 3:19–20).

The period of Jesus also belonged to a time back in the past. His period of history was not the end of history in the sense of cessation or conclusion. But it was the end of history in the sense that it was the unique, decisive period for the realization of God's saving purpose.

The second period, the period of Jesus, extended from the descent of the Holy Spirit upon him at his baptism (Luke 3:22) until the return of the Spirit to God at Jesus' crucifixion (Luke 23:46). During this period Jesus was the only one Luke described as filled with the Holy Spirit. At its beginning Satan was repulsed (Luke 4:1–13) and retired from the scene, inactive (Luke 4:13b). Only near the end of the period of Jesus, when the hostility of the Jewish leaders had intensified into a conspiracy to murder him, did Satan find "the opportune time" in the person of Judas Iscariot to renew his assault on the Spirit-empowered Messiah (Luke 22:3–6).

This second period was the time of the fulfillment of the promises anticipated in the first period (Luke 4:21; 24:44; and frequently in between). It was the time for preaching the kingly rule of God not as expectation but at last as reality (Luke 16:16). It was the middle point of human time, "the hinge of history, in which both the meaning of the past and the course of the future are revealed."[22]

The third period is the epoch of the church. The first and second periods, the times of Israel and of Jesus, were in the distant past. The period of the church embraces the recent past, the present, and the future. It began with the outpouring of the Holy Spirit on believers at Pentecost (Acts 2:1–4; cf. Luke 3:16; 24:49; Acts 1:5, 8), and extends to the second coming of Jesus and the end of the world. It is the time for mission, for proclaiming the good news of what God had revealed as his intent in the first period and has realized in the second period. It is the time to witness to people everywhere in God's creation concerning salvation accomplished (Luke 24:47–48; Acts 1:8). The church is commissioned and empowered to issue the call to repentance, announce the forgiveness of sins, and affirm the promised gift of the Holy Spirit to those who believe (Acts 2:38–39).

It is interesting that Luke described a forty-day period of preparation at the outset of both the second and third periods of salvation history. The period of Jesus began with the forty-day temptation experience in the wilderness (Luke 4:1–13). The prelude to the period of the church was a forty-day association of the disciples with Jesus. This interval includes the resurrection and the post-resurrection appearances, a time of instruction, and the ascension of Jesus into heaven (Luke 24; Acts 1:1–11). Is it merely coincidence that the figure "forty" occurs so often in the inaugural traditions of the first period, the period of Israel, as recorded in the Jewish Scriptures (the flood of Noah lasted forty days—Genesis 7:4; Israel wandered in the wilderness forty years—Exodus 16:35; Moses waited on Mount Sinai forty days—Exodus 24:18)? In Jewish religious symbolism "forty" was a sacred number frequently used to indicate a period of preparation and testing prior to the introduction of a significant new event or stage in salvation history.

5. Gospel to Gentiles

As far as we can tell, Luke was a Gentile Christian whose Christian community was composed predominantly of Gentile Christians. It is not surprising, therefore, to discover a strong interest in the universal scope of the gospel pervading his writings. God intended to save all of his creation including Gentiles. Redemption was not limited just to the Jews. That had an immediate interest for Luke and his community as well as affecting the enthusiasm with which they did missionary preaching.

We encounter specific reference to the Gentiles early in the Gospel. Simeon recognized the infant Jesus as the embodiment of that salvation of God which was both "a glory to thy people Israel" and "a light for revelation to the Gentiles" (Luke 2:32). Luke's genealogy of Jesus did not stop with Abraham, the Father of Israel, but extended on to include Adam, the Father of all humanity (Luke 3:23–38). Following the first incident Luke described in Jesus' public ministry, the preaching at Nazareth (Luke 4:16–22), Jesus drew an analogy to the significance of his own ministry by referring to the prophets Elijah and Elisha whom God sent to minister to non-Jews (Luke 4:24–27).

Jesus' home-town folk, angered by his analogy, sought to kill him (Luke 4:28–29). That anticipated the rejection by the Jews which culminated in his execution. It was precisely their rejection which gave Gentiles access to gospel salvation. The pattern was repeated often in the second volume. The gospel was announced first to the Jews, as God had promised. Though some believed, most didn't. When they rejected the proclamation of the Easter church it directed its preaching to Gentiles. That shift in direction was not simply an "ad hoc" accommodation. The Holy Spirit compelled the universalistic perspective. The church had superseded the Jewish people as true Israel. It was through the disciples and the Jerusalem church that continuity with the salvation history of Israel was maintained unbroken.

6. Lesser Interests

Several other concepts, while not being as important as the ones listed above, figure prominently in Luke's writings.

a. Prayer—Luke was fond of describing Jesus and, in imitation of him, also the disciples, in the posture of prayer. He included many more prayer traditions than did the other evangelists.

b. Sympathy for the Poor—One of the nativity hymns at the beginning of Luke's Gospel anticipated Jesus' concern for the dispossessed (Luke 1:52–53). Twice Jesus appealed to the preaching of good news to the poor as evidence of his messianic identity (Luke 4:18; 7:22). The parables of the rich fool (Luke 12:16–21), of the dishonest steward (Luke 16:1–9), of the rich man and Lazarus (Luke 16:19–31), and the story of Zacchaeus (Luke 19:2–10), all express sympathy for the plight of the poor.

c. Women—Luke included several traditions about women that appear in neither Matthew nor Mark. Besides their obvious importance in the birth and infancy stories (Luke 1—2), women are main actors in several stories from Jesus' public ministry (cf. Luke 7:11–17, 36–50; 8:2, 42–48; 10:38–42; 21:1–4; 23:27–31; 23:55—24:11). The result is that women play a more prominent role in Luke's version of the life of Jesus than they do in the other Gospels.

d. Outcasts and Sinners—Luke emphasized the compassion Jesus exhibited toward those whom religious Judaism regarded as impious and unacceptable to God. Tax collectors, being unscrupulous exploiters of the people of God, were popularly hated as enemies of God. But Jesus not only chose Levi, a tax collector, to be his close associate (Luke 5:27–32), he stayed as guest in Zacchaeus' house in Jericho (Luke 19:2–10) and told the story of a tax collector who was more acceptable to God than a "religious" Pharisee (Luke 18:9–14). Similarly Jesus told stories in which hated Samaritans played exemplary roles which faithful Jews should emulate (Luke 10:29–37; 17:11–19). The force of Luke's emphasis on Jesus' ministry to the despised was to throw in even sharper relief the extraordinary mercy of God.

IV. WHO WAS LUKE AND WHEN DID HE WRITE?

The author of the Third Gospel and of Acts was an anonymous Gentile Christian who was well-educated. According to the preface of the first volume in his two-volume work he considered himself to belong to the third stage of Christianity. "Many have undertaken to compile a narrative of the things . . . delivered to us by those who . . . were eyewitnesses and ministers of the word [and] it seemed good to me . . . to write an orderly account" (Luke 1:1–3).

The eyewitnesses accompanied Jesus during his ministry. In the beginning years of the life of the church they were joined by other ministers of the word. The figures of Stephen, Philip, Barnabas, and Paul as they appear in the Acts narrative are representative of this stage. They stood in continuity with the select group of eyewitnesses who served as the founding nucleus of the primitive church. They passed on the eyewitness traditions through preaching and teaching. The collectors and compilers of the traditions, the third stage, included Mark, whoever was responsible for Q and any other written sources used by Luke, and Luke himself.

Church tradition associated the name of Luke with these writings as early as the latter half of the second century, C.E.[23] All of the early references to "Luke" considered him a colleague of the Apostle Paul. There are several passages in the New Testament which testify that the early church knew traditions of a "Luke" who was Paul's companion (Philem. 24; Col. 4:14; 2 Tim. 4:11). Perhaps, because of the prominent role Paul has in the Acts narrative, those texts stimulated the custom of linking the name of Luke to the anonymous two-volume work. Perhaps the name of Luke had been attached to the writings and then subsequently, because both names were the same, the early church equated them. Nevertheless the work remains anonymous.

Since Luke used the Gospel of Mark as one source, he had to have written later than Mark (c. 65 C.E.). Luke's Gospel seems to reflect knowledge of the seige of Jerusalem and the destruction of the Temple in 70 C.E. (Luke 13:34–35; 19:41–44; 21:20–24). It therefore must have been composed after those events.

Although Luke-Acts is quoted by second century Christian authors it seems probable that the documents were written earlier than that. There is no compelling evidence that Luke used Matthew (written c. 85–90 C.E.), but that should not be emphasized too much. Maybe the Gospel of Matthew was used in only a limited area for some time.

More useful is the recognition that Luke apparently did not know Paul's letters. Disparities in detail concerning the career and theology of Paul in Acts compared to the autobiographical information Paul gave about himself indicate that Acts was written before the epistles of Paul were widely circulated as a collection in early Christianity. This observation is the major obstacle in the identification of the author of Luke-Acts with a companion of Paul. Since Ignatius of Antioch did know such a collection in 110 C.E. and assumed that his reader did also, Luke-Acts probably was written before that. It is difficult to believe that Luke would have either ignored or deliberately contradicted Paul's letters if he knew them.

The strong apologetic tone of Luke-Acts, arguing that Christianity was not a politically subversive movement, suggests that the writing occurred at a time when the Roman authorities had begun to differentiate between Judaism and Christianity. Apparently Rome was becoming suspicious about the objectives of the early church. Stress between Christianity and Imperial Rome intensified during the reign of the Emperor Domitian (81–96 C.E.), a likely period to date the composition of Luke-Acts. That would make this two-volume work roughly contemporaneous with the Gospel of Matthew—written c. 85–90 C.E.

The place where Luke-Acts was composed is undiscoverable. Since it is so thoroughly Greek it seems unlikely that it was written in a community subject to much near-Eastern influence such as would be the case with Palestine or Syria. But more than that cannot be established.

V. OUTLINE

I. Prologue to Luke-Acts 1:1–4

II. Birth and infancy stories 1:5—2:52
  A. Announcements about John the Baptist and Jesus 1:5–56
  B. Births of John the Baptist and Jesus 1:57—2:20
  C. Presentation of infant Jesus 2:21–40
  D. Child Jesus at the Temple 2:41–52

III. Preparation for public ministry 3:1—4:13
  A. Preaching of John the Baptist 3:1–20
  B. Descent of the Holy Spirit 3:21–22
  C. Genealogy 3:23–38
  D. Temptation 4:1–13

IV. Ministry in Galilee 4:14—9:50
  A. Preaching and rejection at Nazareth 4:14–30
  B. Miraculous healings at Capernaum 4:31–44
  C. Call of the first disciples 5:1–11
  D. Conflicts with the Pharisees 5:12—6:11
  E. Call of the Twelve 6:12–16
  F. Sermon on the Plain 6:17–49
  G. Power over sickness and death 7:1–17
  H. John the Baptist and Jesus 7:18–35
  I. Penitent woman with ointment 7:36–50
  J. Wise teachings and marvelous deeds 8:1–56
  K. Mission of the Twelve 9:1–11
  L. Feeding of 5000 9:12–17
  M. Peter's confession and Jesus' prediction of his death 9:18–27
  N. Transfiguration 9:28–36
  O. Defective discipleship 9:37–50

V. Journey toward Jerusalem 9:51—19:27
  A. Hostile Samaritans 9:51–56
  B. Absolute demands of discipleship 9:57–62
  C. Sending of the Seventy 10:1–24
  D. Parable of the Good Samaritan 10:25–37
  E. Mary and Martha 10:38–42
  F. On prayer 11:1–13
  G. On exorcisms 11:14–28

H. On signs 11:29–36
I. Against the Pharisees and scribes 11:37–54
J. On discipleship 12:1—13:9
K. Sabbath activities 13:10–21
L. Reversal of fortune 13:22–35
M. Table-fellowship with a Pharisee 14:1–24
N. Cost of discipleship 14:25–35
O. Concern for the lost 15:1–32
P. On wealth 16:1–31
Q. On faith and duty 17:1–10
R. Healing of ten lepers 17:11–19
S. On the kingdom of god and the Son of man 17:20–37
T. Parables about prayer 18:1–14
U. On entering the kingdom of God 18:15–30
V. Prediction of martyrdom 18:31–34
W. Jesus in Jericho 18:35—19:27

VI. Ministry in Jerusalem 19:28—21:38
A. Triumphal Entry 19:28–40
B. Judgment on Jerusalem 19:41–44
C. Cleansing of the Temple 19:45–46
D. Hostility of Jewish leaders 19:47—20:8
E. Story of the wicked tenants 20:9–18
F. Controversies with Jewish leaders 20:19—21:4
G. Warnings about end-time events 21:5–38

VII. Passion and resurrection 22:1—24:53
A. Conspiracy against Jesus 22:1–6
B. Last Supper 22:7–23
C. Farewell discourse 22:24–38
D. On the Mount of Olives 22:39–46
E. Arrested, denied, and mocked 22:47–65
F. Trials 22:66—23:25
G. Crucifixion 23:26–49
H. Burial 23:50–56
I. Discovery of empty tomb 24:1–12
J. Appearance on road to Emmaus 24:13–35
K. Appearance to disciples 24:36–43
L. Leave-taking and departure 24:44–53

CHAPTER FIVE
Extended Considerations

In the last chapters we have looked together at three documents included in the New Testament of the Bible. The authors of these documents each composed his "Gospel" to provide his own Christian community with a narrative account of the ministry of Jesus. In spite of the fact that all three narratives were not the same (perhaps, even, *because* of that fact), they are all part of the New Testament. Christians today regard the Bible, which contains that New Testament including our Synoptic Gospels, as possessing a special authority for the Christian faith, worship, and life.

Early Christians wrote other documents which also contained stories about Jesus. Yet those documents did not become part of the Bible. Why not? What does it mean for Christians today who do not belong to any of the evangelists' communities, who don't live in their time or culture, who don't even speak their language, to acknowledge the special authority of these writings?

These are some of the questions we will consider in this chapter. First, we will recall together the rich variety of religious experience, of historical context, and of theological expression which early Christians enjoyed. That variety of religious experience led those early Christians to adapt Jesus stories so that they spoke more directly to their different circumstances. How can we be sure, then, which of the

Jesus stories (or which Gospel version of the same story), accurately reports what Jesus actually did or said? How crucial is the demonstration of that accuracy for the authority which the story carries for contemporary Christian faith?

We will next consider some of the early Christian literature which didn't make it into the Bible. That will raise for us the related question about the process followed by the Christian church to decide which Christian documents were to be included in the New Testament. On the basis of our summary overview of the history of that process we will consider the related issues of the continuing authority and inspiration of Scripture for Christians today.

I. DIVERSITY IN NEW TESTAMENT CHRISTIANITY

As we have seen, the authors of the three Synoptic Gospels, Matthew, Mark, and Luke, were all intent on the same basic task. They were interested in fusing the stories of Jesus which were circulating in both oral and written forms into a continuous narrative. Those narratives portrayed the career of Jesus in order to aid early Christians both in strengthening their own faith and as a resource for their missionary preaching and teaching.

During our discussion of the Synoptic Gospels I have tried consistently to refer to the evangelists' *portraits* of Jesus. For they are certainly portraits rather than biographies. That is, the Gospel writers were interested in more than just reporting to their communities anecdotes about Jesus.

Each evangelist shaped the narrative development of his Gospel so that as he told the story of Jesus he caused it to address concerns which were current to his community. The narrative story of Jesus invited its hearers to become themselves participants in that story. That's the way stories function, especially in an oral culture. As the Christian colleagues of the evangelist entered into his story of Jesus they gained new insights into the scope and significance of the issues which were problematic in their own Christian community.

Mark composed his Gospel narrative out of stories of Jesus most of which were already available to his community in oral or written form. It is unlikely that, once the community had access to Mark's

Gospel, that document immediately became their exclusive source for traditions about Jesus. They probably continued using the stories in the forms in which they were already familiar with them for some time. But Mark hoped that, more and more, they would come to depend on his retelling of these stories as they had been fitted into the framework of his Gospel narrative. He believed that his version made the stories of Jesus available to his community in a less ambiguous, less confusing, and therefore more useful, form. He told the stories of Jesus better. He intended for the stories of Jesus as he told them in his Gospel eventually to take the place of other versions of those stories current in his own Christian community.

Mark's church, however, was only one small segment of early Christianity. His own Christian colleagues did become more appreciative of his work and depended on it. But lots of other Christians didn't even know Mark's version, and still continued to tell (and even to modify) the stories about Jesus as they knew them in their oral form. Only gradually did Mark's Gospel gain a wider audience.

Eventually Mark's Gospel came to be used by Luke's community also, although Mark did not have that community and its problems in mind when he wrote it. As we have already seen in chapter 4, Luke revised and expanded Mark's Gospel so that his version of the story of Jesus would address specific needs and concerns of his own community. It was not that Mark had not done a good job. But Luke thought he could do it better, at least for his local church. Although he could not expect it to happen immediately, Luke intended that his version of the narrative of Jesus' life and death eventually would supplant Mark's as a resource for his community.

What we have just said about the intentions of both Mark and Luke to replace with their own writings those forms of the stories of Jesus which were already familiar to their communities we may also apply to Matthew. Even then we are taking into account only three segments of early Christianity. The Matthean and Lukan communities overlapped that segment of the early Christian church which was using Mark, as they also did the segment using Q. There were other large groups of Christians who did not know or, at least did not depend on any of the three Synoptic Gospels in the New Testament. Many Christians still knew the stories of Jesus only as they were being passed on in the oral tradition. They continued to modify those stories to speak to their needs.

A group like this is the Johannine Christian community. It produced the Gospel of John and the Johannine epistles. Scholars are not at all convinced that the Johannine segment of early Christianity knew any of the three Synoptic Gospels. They certainly knew some of the same stories, for example the Cleansing of the Temple (John 2:13–22), or the Miraculous Feeding (John 6:1–14), or Peter's Denial (John 18:15–18, 25–27). But their version of the ministry of Jesus has been accommodated to their needs and interests, and thoroughly recast in their special vocabulary. The points of contact between their story of Jesus' life and those of the Synoptic Gospels are scant.

The Gospel of John is another good example within the New Testament of the adaptation of stories of Jesus which originally circulated as oral traditions. The Johannine community composed its modified version of the story of Jesus independent from the Synoptic Gospels. It was not intended to replace any one of them. When we look at the types of early Christian literature outside of the New Testament we will note some other examples of this phenomenon.

What we have been observing on the basis of our consideration of the Gospels in the New Testament is the rich diversity of ways early Christians thought about Jesus, and the widely varying problems to which they applied the stories they had heard about him. It is important that we recognize this variety in early Christianity. Much Bible study tends to obscure that variety. Many scholars are interested in describing *the* New Testament view of things (for example, *the* New Testament doctrine of the church, or, *the* New Testament concept of grace, or, *the* New Testament baptism), as if there were only one opinion in all of the New Testament documents on these topics. Out of that interest they overlook the rich pluralism of religious views recorded by the various New Testament writers. Their amalgamation of all New Testament opinions into one New Testament concept blurs the distinctiveness of individual perspective that makes the New Testament collection of literature so fascinating.[1]

This diversity of perspective is not limited to the different ways the Gospel writers told their narratives of Jesus. It permeates all of the New Testament literature. There is pluralistic diversity in the preaching of early Christians, in the ways they worshiped, in the institutional structures they devised to govern their community life, as well as in a host of other features reflected in the New Testament documents. To pursue them all is beyond the scope of our task.[2] But that does broaden the perspective over against which we perceive the diversity present in the evangelists' presentations.

The widespread popularity which each of the Gospels eventually enjoyed far surpassed the modest goals for which the evangelists originally composed them. Mark did not write his Gospel with the view that the Christian communities to which Matthew and Luke belonged would also make use of it. He wrote his Gospel for his community. In the same manner neither Matthew nor Luke, nor for that matter, the Johannine community, was consciously addressing a broad range of differing situations within which first century Christians found themselves. Much less could they have conceived, in their most extreme fantasies, twenty centuries of continuous use of their documents by generations of Christians. They were simply writing their Gospels for their communities.

When Christians later did make a wider use of the Gospels they were employing them for purposes and situations beyond the uses for which they were originally designed. That is to say, the later church discovered a broader and more universal usefulness in the Gospels' narratives than the evangelists intended when they composed them.

Have you ever wondered what happened when members of Luke's community, who had been using his Gospel as their exclusive source for the Jesus stories for a considerable time, expanded their missionary preaching into a new region only to discover that Christians from Mark's community, who continued to regard his Gospel as *the* story of Jesus, were already active there? Or what do you think happened when some of the Johannine community first met Christians who had been nurtured on the Gospel of Matthew? Only remarkable openness prevented later Christians from being severely disturbed by the various ways in which the evangelists employed the Jesus stories. Nor were they troubled by the diverse perspectives about Jesus which the several Gospel narratives presented. There was a tolerance in their appreciation which encouraged them to embrace the pluralism of perspectives. They received the differences not as contradictions but as enriching diversity. So they did not feel compelled to grant exclusive authority to one at the expense of the suppression of the others. While the evangelists intended in some instances to supplant earlier versions the later church related them side by side as enrichingly complementary.

II. THE QUEST FOR THE HISTORICAL JESUS

We have already seen that Mark, Matthew, and Luke, and those Christians before and after them who continued to rely on the oral tradition selected stories of Jesus and modified them to apply to their own community situations. That recognition raises an important problem. How can we tell which of these versions most accurately report what Jesus really did and said during his earthly ministry? Which ones of the large collection of the stories about Jesus which they incorporated into the Gospels relate authentic historical witness?

Although that is a problem for us it is a problem which only recently has been identified. For hundreds of years the question wasn't even raised. Christians assumed that the four Gospels were reverent biographies of Jesus composed by those who were present and observed directly the events they were recording. Or, at least, the authors were intimate friends and colleagues of the eyewitnesses and had immediate access to their recollections.

On the basis of those assumptions it was a popular project of biblical scholars to put together a composite biography of Jesus. They tried to write an account of his life by combining the information of each of the Gospels into one continuous narrative. These attempts became the most numerous during the nineteenth century. There are those who still try to do this.

An embarrassment of this enterprise is the difference in the "lives of Jesus" which modern authors reconstruct out of the canonical Gospels. No two are alike. We may account for that striking discrepancy partially because not only are there different Jesus traditions included in each of the four Gospels but also when the same stories are present they are reported in a different sequence or in differing forms.

The different interpretations by the evangelists of who Jesus was, and what he was about, and the impact which that had on their diverse religious concerns comprised a more fundamental impediment to the production of a universally recognized and accepted life of Jesus. Those varying interpretations cannot be combined so that each receives equal emphasis. Anyone who tries to write a life of Jesus must select one biblical interpretation to which the writer subordinates the others. The subjectivity of the modern author rather than the data in New Testament documents themselves determines that selection.[3]

Scholars reacted against the naive overconfidence of nineteenth century writers that they could reconstruct an accurate biography of Jesus from the traditions in the Gospels. There were those who held that very little information at all could be recovered about the Jesus of history. Further, they claimed, lack of access to data about the historical Jesus really didn't matter. The Christian faith was fundamentally molded by the conviction of the earliest Christians that Jesus had been raised from the dead. That conviction irreversibly colored their telling of the stories of Jesus. But that wasn't so serious because information about what occurred to Jesus before was irrelevant to modern interests. Christianity had its roots in the apostolic faith.

Recently scholarly voices have been raised to protest both previous extremes. Although an extensive biographical reconstruction of the ministry of Jesus isn't possible, more data about Jesus' earthly life was recoverable than their predecessors had allowed. The extraordinary impact which the person, Jesus, had on subsequent world history evokes a genuine and legitimate historical curiosity about his life. Beyond that, however, it was more important for Christian theology than the earlier scholars had recognized.

First, Christianity, as well as Judaism, has placed high value on its conviction that God encounters humanity by entering into and being active within human history. Recovery of historical data about Jesus would nurture that conviction. Second, it is true that the primary source for Christian theology is the apostolic faith. But that faith was formed precisely as the earliest Christians reflected on the impressions they had received of Jesus when they were associated with him, and revised them in the light of their conviction that God had raised him from the dead. Easter was a wholly new surprise for the ways they had come to think about Jesus up until then. Yet they affirmed a continuity which transcended that surprise. Recovery of historical data from the ministry of Jesus promised to provide perspectives external to and prior to the origins of the apostolic faith. Those perspectives would help us comprehend something of the reasons and the process which produced the apostolic faith with its unique features.

The difficulty in establishing authentic historical reminiscence for the stories of Jesus contained in the Gospels lies in the form in which we have access to them.

The Gospel of John appears to have been the last of the four Gospels written in the New Testament. Scholars agree that that Gospel has reworked its Jesus traditions to reflect Johannine theological interests more thoroughly than the other canonical Gospels reworked their traditions. That does not mean that no historical data is present in the Gospel of John. (That is the only Gospel, for instance, which clearly portrays the ministry of Jesus as extending over three years. Yet scholars regard that period of time much more likely than the one year interval implied by the Synoptic Gospels.) Nevertheless, the demonstration of the historicity of data in the Gospel of John is extremely difficult.

As we have seen already, both Matthew and Luke used the Gospel of Mark as one of their sources. That means that the Gospel of Mark contains stories of Jesus in the earliest possible form to which we have direct access. Yet, as we saw in chapter 1, significant modifications had been made to those stories before Mark heard them, and he made additional changes when he incorporated them into his document (chapter 2). The only thing we can say for sure is what those stories looked like after Mark had built them into his narrative.[4] Anything we say about the pre-Markan form of the stories is conjecture. We can talk only about "probabilities" then, not "certainties."

Accepting the limitations which the nature of our sources thrusts upon us, how do we go about the task of establishing the "probability" of historical data in a story about Jesus? What kind of questions must we ask to discover those strands of early Christian tradition which have a strong claim to historical accuracy? Scholars have so far described three.[5]

A. Criterion of Dissimilarity

The most important test which scholars have defined to identify the probability of the presence of historical data is the criterion of dissimilarity. This test holds that first we have to determine the earliest form we can identify of a saying or other story about Jesus. We may then consider that tradition as an anecdote reporting an authentic occurrence in the ministry of Jesus *if* it can be shown to be dissimilar to characteristic emphases of first century Judaism and of the early (pre-Markan) Christian church.

Why must it be dissimilar to characteristic emphases of the early church? We have already observed several times that early Christians selected those Jesus stories to pass on which were the most helpful to them in their preaching and teaching. As they encountered different situations they modified the stories to address those new circumstances. Any time a story about Jesus reflects features which typically interested the earliest Christians we can never be sure whether we are hearing an anecdote that really happened or a story that was molded to speak to a concern which emerged in early Christianity.

Why must the story be dissimilar, then, to characteristic emphases of first century Judaism? We need to remind ourselves that, as far as we can tell, the earliest Christians were Jews who continued to participate in the Jewish worship, to observe its holy days and festivals and to keep the Mosaic law. They assimilated many practices and attitudes which were part of the contemporary Jewish piety and morality. Those features shaped aspects of their faith and their community life over which, they were convinced, the exalted Jesus ruled. It was natural for them to cast justification for those practices into the form of Jesus sayings in order to commend them to new members of their fellowship.

Let us look at a couple of examples to demonstrate the considerable amount of historical data which we can recover with strong probability by employing the criterion of dissimilarity.

Mark summarized the content of Jesus' preaching as "The time is fulfilled, and the kingdom of God is at hand; repent, and believe in the gospel" (Mark 1:15). Several of the individual sayings of Jesus reported in the Gospels reflect that same emphasis on the presence of the kingdom of God. For example, "The kingdom of God is not coming with signs to be observed; nor will they say, 'Lo, here it is!' or 'There!' for behold, the kingdom of God is in the midst of you" (Luke 17:20–21).

That proclamation of the present inauguration of the kingly rule of God in his creation is dissimilar to the central concerns of first century Jewish piety. The Jews in Jesus' day anticipated that God would eventually restore his kingly rule over his creation on Mount Zion. But they were mainly convinced that that event would take place in the far distant future. Hardly anyone expected for it to happen soon, much less right then. They were warily suspicious of any religious fanatic who suggested it.

The proclamation of the inbreaking of the kingdom of God was also demonstrably distinct from the primary interests of early Christians. The central content of the proclamation of most of them was not the kingdom of God but Jesus himself. They preached the cross event, Jesus' crucifixion and resurrection, as that mighty act of divine intervention by which God renewed his creation and confirmed the identity of Jesus as Messiah and Lord.

Therefore we may regard the Lukan report that Jesus announced "The kingdom of God is in your midst" as quite probably an accurate recollection of something Jesus really said during his earthly ministry. It should be stressed that we are speaking only of "probabilities" here —and that will be so with the other two criteria we will discuss, too. The only "certainties" we have are the forms of the Jesus stories as they currently exist incorporated into the narratives of the New Testament Gospels.

Let us consider another example of the application of the criterion of dissimilarity. In Mark's description of Jesus in Gethsemane, Jesus addressed his prayer to God calling him "Abba" (Mark 14:36).[6] Since that is an Aramaic word it would certainly seem to Greek-speaking Gentile Christians to be a strange word to call God. As we can see in Mark's text he has to translate it, "Abba, Father," so his readers can understand it. Both Matthew and Luke omit the Aramaic word in their versions and retain only Mark's translation, "Father."

Since "Abba" is an Aramaic word we know that it could not have originated in Hellenistic Christianity. This tradition goes back at least to the earliest stages of Christianity when most Christians were still Aramaic-speaking Jews. Even in that context "Abba" would seem to many a strange, even offensive, way to address God. The word "Abba" was an expression of intimate endearment. It was the term small children used to call to their fathers. The closest analogy which we have in English is "Daddy." No pious first century Jew, schooled as they all were to hold God in awesome respect and holy fear, would have dared call him "Abba." (Not many of us would be comfortable praying to God, especially in public, and calling him "Daddy.") That term as a way of addressing God is clearly dissimilar to the customs of first century Jewish piety.

Since the first, Aramaic-speaking Christians, would have shared the same religious background and conditioning as their non-Christian Jewish counterparts, it is equally unlikely that they would have decided to call God "Abba" on their own initiative, much less put that startling term into the mouth of Jesus. The term was dissimilar to the earliest Christian religious instincts, also. Only a person exercising extraordinary authority could induce them by his example to call God "Abba." Only Jesus could have been the one responsible for introducing into Christian vocabulary this term which expressed both intimate devotion and filial obedience.

B. Criterion of Multiple Attestation

The criterion of dissimilarity is not the only clue by which we can identify with reasonable probability stories which transmit accurate recollections out of the life and ministry of Jesus. Another test pointing to authentic reminiscence is the criterion of multiple attestation. According to this criterion we may regard as probably authentic any theme, motif, or saying which occurs in several different forms of the oral tradition (for example, a pronouncement saying, a parable, and an independent logion). This test also applies if we find the same material contained in several different sources which the Gospel writers used (for example, in the Gospel of Mark, and in Q, and in the Gospel of John).

Let us consider an example of the application of this criterion. The motif that Jesus showed special compassionate concern for the outcast, for tax collectors, and sinners occurs frequently in the four canonical Gospels. The criterion of multiple attestation would suggest to us that that motif reports a real dimension in Jesus' ministry. It occurs in a variety of forms (pronouncement stories, miracle stories, parables, etc.) and in multiple Gospel sources (Mark, Q, M, L, the Gospel of John).

C. Criterion of Coherence

Scholars have defined yet a third test by which they seek to identify recollections of probably genuine events in Jesus' life. This third criterion is the test of coherence or consistency. Its successful use depends on the results obtained from the first two criteria. It builds on the authentic traditions which we are able to identify and to accumulate from their application.

The criterion of coherence encourages us to reconsider additional stories of Jesus even though their genuineness appears dubious, or at least ambiguous, when we apply the two criteria of dissimilarity and of multiple attestation. According to this test they may be regarded as probably historical if they can be shown to be consistent with traditions which the first two criteria have suggested are genuine remembrances. They are compatible with those authentic remembrances and therefore cohere to them.

To illustrate the application of this criterion let us recall our previous discussion of the use which the Gospel of Mark ascribes to Jesus of the term "Abba" as a word to address God. We saw that that use was demonstrably distinct from the customs of first century Jewish piety and of earliest, Aramaic-speaking, Jewish Christianity.[7]

There are a number of other traditions in which Jesus is described as calling God "Father" or as alluding to God as his father, but in which he does not use the term "Abba." (We can understand how the term would eventually fall into disuse as Christianity became more and more focused toward Greek-speaking Gentiles.) Nevertheless the criterion of coherence would accumulate all of those "Father" sayings which reflect the sense of filial intimacy combined with loving obedience which "Abba" expressed. It would encourage us to regard them as having a very strong claim to authenticity. They are consistent with and cohere to the "Abba" tradition.

We may observe an interesting extension of the use of the criterion of coherence as it evaluates a saying of Jesus which is not in our New Testament Gospels. One ancient (sixth century) manuscript of the New Testament contains this additional saying inserted after Luke 6:4:

> "On the same day he saw a man working on the sabbath and said to him, 'Man, if you know what you are doing, you are blessed; but if you do not know, you are accursed and a transgressor of the law.' "[8]

The saying clearly was not a part of the original version of the Gospel of Luke or we would find it included in more than just one of the ancient Greek manuscripts. (Around 5,000 have been found.) Our four evangelists either didn't know that saying or chose to exclude it from their narratives. It was one of the sayings of Jesus which continued to be told in the oral tradition. Apparently a sixth century scribe who knew the oral version of this saying was copying the Gospel of Luke. He inserted the saying into the text because it dealt with the same topic, sabbath observance, as did the traditions Luke had included at that point in his narrative.

The criterion of coherence would encourage us to regard that inserted saying as an authentic quotation of Jesus. As Norman Perrin observes "it coheres perfectly with something that has multiple attestation in the canonical tradition: the challenge of Jesus to make one's own decisions."[9] As far as we can tell Jesus probably really said that saying.[10]

D. Limitations and Results of the Quest

We have just considered three criteria which assist us to move behind the documents in our New Testament and the oral traditions they incorporated to recognize genuine data descriptive of Jesus' ministry. As helpful as these tests of the tradition are, they do have their limits.

The most obvious defect with the criterion of dissimilarity is its demand for demonstrable distinctiveness. Surely there must have been a great deal in the ministry and teaching of Jesus which corresponded to features of contemporary Jewish piety. It also seems very likely that earliest Christianity faithfully appropriated and extended aspects of Jesus' ministry as integral components of its religious perspective. In both of these instances the criterion of dissimilarity not only doesn't expose the authenticity of these traditions, it deliberately directs our attention away from them.

We must acknowledge a second qualification that applies in varying degrees to all three criteria. Each of the criteria presumes that we are accurately informed about first century Jewish piety, earliest Christianity, and the subsequent stages through which Christianity moved before the documents which we know as our canonical Gospels were written.

Unfortunately we are not that well-informed at all. We know a great deal about the first century and are continuing to learn more. But there is very much that we still do not know. Some of the judgments we make about historical accuracy on the basis of our criteria may well be defective not because the criteria do not work but because of our ignorance. As we learn more, scholars will correct such ill-informed blunders.

We should list a third qualification for the sake of completeness. We probably don't know all of the criteria, the tests, by which we can identify authentic historical reminiscence. Scholarship surely will define some additional questions that we may address to the Jesus traditions in our canonical Gospels to increase our fund of data about the historical Jesus.

In all this we must acknowledge that we are not making negative judgments about the worth or dependability of the information contained in the Gospels material. Rather we are describing the limits to our current methodology.

The results which have been gained already by the use of the three criteria we have been investigating are not inconsiderable. The consensus among scholars who have been applying these criteria to the Jesus traditions is that we may recognize authentic reminiscence in the large number of stories describing Jesus as proclaiming the inauguration of God's kingly rule, in most of the parables and in the group of traditions that cluster around the "Abba" and the "Lord's Prayer" traditions. They also include main events in the life of Jesus such as his baptism, his ministry in Galilee, the trip to Jerusalem, his arrest, trial, and crucifixion.[11]

III. EXTRA-CANONICAL LITERATURE

We have seen that the oral transmission of the stories about Jesus by early Christians is one presupposition we must make to account for the composition of the four Gospels. Those stories were being recounted both before the Gospels were written and while the Gospels were being written, and they continued to be passed on orally in major segments of early Christianity after the written Gospels were completed.

Early Christians could not have anticipated that later on the church would set aside the Gospels of Matthew, Mark, Luke, and John into a special category approved for general use. For that matter they could not have forseen that the other twenty-three documents would eventually be gathered together with those Gospels to comprise our New Testament. They continued to write letters to other Christians, to preach sermons, and to retell the stories of Jesus, repeatedly adapting them in much the same way and for many of the same reasons as we have observed our evangelists doing.

A. The Apostolic Fathers

Some of those ancient documents which were written by early Christians but which were not included in the New Testament have survived.

The "Apostolic Fathers" is one collection of such literature. These documents were not gathered together under that title until quite recently. (One of them, the Didache, was not discovered until 1883.) Nonetheless, some of them were written about the same time as our later New Testament documents. Scholars date them in the late first and early second centuries. They include the writings attributed to Clement, Ignatius, Polycarp, Barnabas, and Hermas, together with the Martyrdom of Polycarp, the Didache, and the Papias fragments. Some lists also include the Epistle to Diognetus and the Quadratus fragment.

The content of these documents varies. Ignatius, a church leader (bishop) of Antioch in Syria, was martyred in Rome around 110 C.E. As he was being taken to Rome to be executed he wrote seven epistles (letters) to Christian communities and their leaders. Those letters give us helpful glimpses into the life and worship of Christian communities at the turn of the century much as the epistles of Paul provided for churches in his day.

I Clement is a letter written by a church leader in Rome to the church in Corinth. II Clement is a sermon urging Christians to repentance and to exercise moral self-control. The Didache combines a manual for ethical advice with instructions concerning worship practices. The Shepherd of Hermas is a popularized presentation of Christian teaching and advice communicated through long, repetitive series of visions, commands, and similitudes. We have a novelistically embellished story of the execution of an early Christian church leader for his faith in the Martyrdom of Polycarp (the Bishop of Smyrna).[12]

This collection of literature greatly increases our knowledge about the development of post-apostolic Christianity. Early Christians held these documents in great veneration. For example, a fourth century Greek manuscript of the Bible[13] includes the Epistle of Barnabas and the Shepherd of Hermas in addition to the books which are in today's New Testament. Apparently the community for which that Bible was prepared considered those documents to be as important as the others. I Clement is included in a twelfth century Syriac manuscript of the New Testament. Its presence there suggests that those Christians had used I Clement as a resource for teaching and preaching, and had ascribed to it a reverent authority similar to the authority they acknowledge in the rest of their New Testament documents for over one thousand years.

B. The New Testament Apocrypha

Scholars have gathered an even larger collection of early Christian literature under the term "New Testament Apocrypha." The term "apocrypha" is derived from a Greek word which meant "hidden." It was first used to refer to documents whose use was restricted only to a few people. They were the elite group who were "spiritual" enough to have access to the mysteries contained in the documents. But the writings were "hidden" from the rest. Later the term was expanded to include all extra-canonical literature (except the Apostolic Fathers). It is in that later, expanded sense that we use the term today.

The New Testament Apocrypha consists of Christian writings, the oldest of which date back as early as 150 C.E. (though we don't have any copies of them that old). These documents are patterned superficially after the types of documents in our New Testament. So there are gospels, acts, epistles, and apocalypses.[14]

Some of this literature was produced by Christians who held beliefs that were later condemned and suppressed by the majority church. Such a group was the Ebionite Christians who considered observance of the Jewish religious laws to be a necessary component of the Christian faith. Another large and influential group were the Gnostic Christians who cast their theological beliefs into a system of secret teachings by which the gnostic ("knowing") adherent gained access to divinity.

Later Christianity did its best to eliminate all traces of these heretical ("not orthodox") beliefs. So we have been dependent for much of our information about them to references and brief quotations of their literature in the writings of Christian authors who argue against them. The portions of their literature which are preserved in the New Testament Apocrypha provide us with a correcting perspective to the bias against them. Our fund of Christian Gnostic writings has been dramatically increased recently as we will discuss below.

Other literature included in the New Testament Apocrypha was the product of popular Christian piety and curiosity. As time went on Christians wondered about people who were mentioned only briefly in the old Christian traditions. They let their imaginations fill in what might have happened in what they considered were gaps in the stories about Jesus and the earliest church. Such fictionalized embellishments and expansions stimulated popular interest. They were pious attempts to novelize. Such efforts to improve on the New Testament narratives are artless for the most part and suffer badly by comparison with the restraint of the earlier stories.

Popular speculation about the missionary careers of the apostles produced works such as the Acts of John, the Acts of Peter, the Acts of Andrew, the Acts of Thomas. The Acts of Paul provides us with an account (fictional) of Paul's execution[15] thereby rectifying the lack in the canonical Acts of the Apostles. Christian apocalypses such as those of Peter, Paul, and Thomas responded to popular curiosity about judgment and punishment in the other world. One of them, the Ascension of Isaiah, portrays a central prophetic figure from the Old Testament bearing explicit testimony to Jesus and to the church. The New Testament Apocrypha contains epistles (letters) purportedly written by Paul to the Laodiceans and to the Corinthians (in addition to the two we have in our New Testament). It also provides an entire series of correspondence between Paul and the philosopher Seneca.

Of particular interest to us, in the light of our previous consideration of the Gospels in our New Testament, are the apocryphal gospels. The New Testament Apocrypha contains a large number of these "gospels."[16] Their titles vary. Some carry the name of individual apostles, some are ascribed to the Twelve, some are named for the communities for which they were composed, some carry names of heretics, some the name of Jesus, some have names of holy women, some just general titles.

Several apocryphal gospels are general theological treatises and have little if anything to do with the type of stories about Jesus we find in the New Testament Gospels. The Gospel of Truth and the Gospel of Philip are like this. The Gospel of Thomas, however, is a collection of 114 sayings of Jesus without any narrative stories at all. Some of the sayings reproduce sayings of Jesus also contained in our canonical Gospels, some are variations of canonical traditions, some are completely different.

When a saying of Jesus in an apocryphal gospel has its counterpart in the New Testament Gospels the contrast is instructive. By comparing the versions we may observe the changes and adaptations which later Christians imposed upon the tradition. Compare the Parable of the Lost Sheep in the Gospel of Matthew (Matt. 18:12–14) and in the Gospel of Luke (Luke 15:3–7) with the Gospel of Thomas version (G. Thom. Logion 107)! (See figure 2.)

The following passage from the apocryphal Gospel of Peter illustrates well the interest evidenced in the apocryphal literature for explicit descriptions of events to which the New Testament documents only allude. As we all know there is no direct description of the resurrection of Jesus in the New Testament. The Gospel of Peter provides one, thereby filling that gap:

> Now in the night in which the Lord's day dawned, when the soldiers, two by two in every watch, were keeping guard, there rang out a loud *voice in heaven,* and they saw the *heavens opened* and two men *come down* from there in a great brightness and draw nigh to the sepulchre. That *stone* which had been laid against the entrance to the sepulchre started of itself *to roll* and gave way to the side, and the sepulchre was opened, and both the young men entered in. When now those soldiers saw this, they awakened the centurion and the elders—for they also were there to assist at the watch. And whilst they were relating what they had seen, they saw again three men come out from the sepulchre, and two of them sustaining the other, and a cross following them, and the heads of the two reaching to heaven, but that of him who was led of them by the hand overpassing the heavens. And they heard a voice out of the heavens crying, "Thou hast preached to them that sleep," and from the cross there was heard the answer, "Yea."[18]

All Christians place great value on the stories about the birth of Jesus. Early Christians found particular fascination in the infancy and childhood of Jesus, since the earliest traditions told so little about those periods of his life. Birth and infancy stories abound in the apocryphal literature. We find even entire works, the infancy gospels, devoted to this interest.

The infancy Gospel of Thomas (not to be confused with the gnostic collection of Jesus sayings also known as the Gospel of Thomas) recounts a series of miracles which the child Jesus supposedly performed.One describes the five-year-old Jesus making twelve clay sparrows. When he was criticized for making them on the sabbath he clapped his hands and they flew away. In another account, when he was six years old, he broke a pitcher accidently so he filled his garment with water and carried it to his mother. There are other tales more sensational than these. The document concludes with an expanded and exaggerated reworking of the story of the twelve-year-old Jesus

Parable of the Lost Sheep

Matthew	*Luke*	*Thomas*[17]
What do you think? If a man has a hundred sheep, and one of them has gone astay,	What man of you, having a hundred sheep if he has lost one of them,	Jesus said: The kingdom is like a shepherd who had a hundred sheep. One of them went astray. It was the largest. He left the ninety-nine (and) sought for one until he found it.
does he not leave the ninety-nine on the hills and go in search of the one that went astray? And if he finds it, truly I say to you,	does not leave the ninety-nine in the wilderness, and go after the one which is lost until he finds it? And when he has found it he lays it on his shoulders, rejoicing, and when he comes home, he calls together his friends and neighbors, saying to them, "Rejoice with me, for I have found my sheep which was lost."	
he rejoices over it		
more than over the ninety-nine that never went astray.	Just so, I tell you, there will be more joy in heaven over one sinner who repents than over ninety-nine righteous persons who need no repentance.	After he had exerted himself, he said to the sheep, I love you more than the ninety-nine.
So, it is not the will of my Father who is in heaven that one of these little ones should perish		

in the Temple of Jerusalem. (We have a more restrained version of the same story in Luke 2:41–51.)

An infancy gospel which has had a visible impact on popular Christian piety to this day is the Protoevangelium of James. It has provided the stimulus for a number of features associated with devotion to Mary, the mother of Jesus. This work concerns itself with stories about events preceding and including the birth of Jesus and Herod's slaughter of the innocents. Its stories include Mary's extraordinary birth to Joachim and Anna, her presentation and service in the Temple, her miraculously arranged betrothal to Joseph, and the birth of Jesus in a cave (instead of a stable). Many medieval paintings of the Nativity reflect this tradition.

C. The Nag Hammadi Documents

Before leaving the subject of literature written by early Christians which was not included in the Bible we should take note of an important recent discovery. In December 1945, two Egyptian farmers, digging fertilizer, found a jar which contained ancient books. They were mostly Gnostic Christian in content. The village of Nag Hammadi nearby provided the name for the discovery. The subsequent history of the books is very complicated and, at points, obscure. Eventually most of them were collected at the Coptic Museum in Cairo.

The library which the farmers found consisted of thirteen codices (codex=book) which contained fifty-two tractates, or literary works, some quite brief but some extensive. In addition to treatises on Gnostic Christian beliefs ("The Interpretation of Knowledge," "The Treatise on Resurrection," "The Exegesis on the Soul," etc.) complete texts of documents known previously only by a few fragments (The Gospel of Thomas, The Gospel of Philip, etc.) were there. Also a large number of hitherto unknown apocryphal documents (The Gospel of Truth, The Teachings of Sylvanus, The Apocalypse of James, etc.) have been added to the collection we knew before the discovery.[19]

The library was collected by an early group of Gnostic Christians who buried them around 400 C.E. to preserve them from some grave threat, probably an invading Roman army. The documents are Coptic translations (an old Egyptian dialect) of Greek texts. The original manuscripts of some of them apparently were composed as far back as the latter part of the second century, C.E.

This rich resource will greatly aid our understanding of Gnostic Christianity. It will also help us appreciate the process and the extent of adaptation of the Jesus traditions by early Christians.

IV. THE CANON OF THE NEW TESTAMENT

Let us now recall several observations we have made earlier in this study. Mark did not write his Gospel with the intent that other Christians besides those of his own community would use his work. But they did. Neither Matthew nor Luke anticipated readers and hearers beyond their own churches. But there have been many. None of them, Mark, Matthew, or Luke, had any inkling they were writing part of the Bible. In the years following their compositions numerous other Christians also wrote documents which related traditions and stories about Jesus.

When were the four Gospels which we have in our New Testament separated out from the larger body of early Christian literature? Why did the early church set them apart? What effect does that decision made by early Christians have on the way we regard those documents today?

All of these questions relate to the process of the formation of the canon of the Bible. "Canon" is a term taken from the Hebrew word for reed. A reed could be cut into specific lengths, therefore, by extension, the word came to mean "a measure, a standard." (The word "cannon" also comes from the same root word for reed but is an extended application of its nature as a hollow tube.) The term "canon" as it is applied to the Bible refers to the list(s) of books (documents) which have come to be regarded as normative for religious belief.

The "Bible" of the earliest Christians was the Jewish Scriptures. As Mark, Matthew, Luke, and the other New Testament authors were composing their documents the collection of writings which they and their communities considered authoritative was the Jewish Scriptures. It is to that body of literature that the writer of 2 Timothy 3:16 was referring when he wrote, "All scripture is inspired by God and profitable for teaching, for reproof, for correction, and for training in righteousness." That was the Scripture Christians read in public worship (1 Timothy 4:13).

But in the earliest decades of Christianity that collection of authoritative Jewish Scriptures had not been completed yet. The Jews were still struggling with decisions about which books should be included. Some sections were complete. The Torah (the Pentateuch—the first five books of the Bible) had long been recognized by Jews as uniquely authoritative. The collection of the oracles of the Prophets had also been completed, and the Jews did not expect for any more of that type of literature to be written. It was the scope of the third section of their collection of sacred books that was in dispute. What documents should be included in the Writings (this category included poetry such as the Psalms, Song of Solomon, and wisdom literature like Ecclesiastes, Job, Wisdom of Solomon, etc.)? Two different lists eventually emerged toward the end of the first century, C.E. The Greek-speaking Jews living outside of Palestine included more documents in their list than were in the list which was drawn up for the Aramaic-speaking Jews by their rabbis.

Early Christians adopted the list drafted by the Greek-speaking Jews. But, as we have seen, they supplemented those Scriptures with the stories about Jesus which had their roots in the eyewitness testimony of the earliest disciples. We have tried in this book to reconstruct the process of the development of those traditions. In the course of that process those stories became more prominent for early Christians who ascribed increasing authority to them.

The written versions of the stories of Jesus enjoyed widening circulation. Other Christian communities than those for whom the Gospels were written became acquainted with them and adopted one or more of them as the standard version(s) for their communities' use. Additional versions containing new and transparently fictional stories about Jesus (the apocryphal gospels) appeared. The eyewitness disciples to whom appeal could be made for authoritative correction and interpretation were dying off. Christians were faced with the need to discriminate between the various documents in the expanding mass of early Christian literature. It was a very practical problem. Which versions of the Jesus stories should receive more emphasis in Christian preaching and teaching? What Christian writings were appropriate to read aloud in public worship along with the readings from the Jewish Scriptures? Which documents should Christians regard as a standard (a measure, a "canon") to which they could appeal in disputed cases of doctrine or discipline?

The separation process was gradual and undesigned. It was in the form of limited collections that early Christians first circulated to wider Christian audiences the documents which they believed were more important. The letters of Paul appear to have been one of the earliest of those collections. (Though, as we have seen, the Gospels in our New Testament are, themselves, early collections of stories of Jesus gathered from different sources.) One of the documents in the Apostolic Fathers, 1 Clement (written about 90 C.E.), appeals to Paul's letters and implies that their authority is similar to the authority of the Jewish Scriptures. Two others of the Apostolic Fathers, Ignatius of Antioch and Polycarp of Smyrna, both had knowledge of collections of Paul's letters. So did the author of 2 Peter. His document, which is included in the New Testament, was written about 125–130 C.E. In it he wrote:

> So also our beloved brother Paul wrote to you according to the wisdom given him, speaking of this [the forbearance of the Lord] as he does in all his letters. There are some things in them hard to understand, which the ignorant and unstable twist to their own destruction, as they do the other scriptures. (2 Peter 3:15–16)

(By "other scriptures" he probably intended a reference to the Jewish Scriptures.)

We find evidence that several Gospels were known in one locale in the later Christian writings. We have already seen that the Gospel of Mark must have been widely distributed quite early since both Matthew and Luke apparently used a copy of that Gospel as a source when they wrote their Gospels. About the time that 2 Peter, which we cited above, was being written, a church leader named Papias in Hieropolis (in what is, today, west-central Turkey), described the

Gospel of Mark and also a collection of Jesus sayings, written in Aramaic, which he associated with the name of Matthew. Although Papias had very high regard for those documents, still he preferred the oral tradition. In his studies he inquired into what the presbyters reported that the Apostles had said about Jesus "for I did not imagine that things out of books would help me as much as the utterances of a living and abiding voice."[20]

Toward the latter part of the second century C.E., we find Christian authors citing passages often from the Gospels of Matthew, Luke, and John, but only infrequently from the Gospel of Mark. This has led scholars to suggest that Mark's Gospel may have fallen into disuse for a period in second century Christianity. We do find a Christian author named Tatian in 172 C.E. trying to combine all four of the Gospels in the New Testament into one. He called his composite the Diatesseron (which means "[one] through the four"). He hoped it would replace the four Gospels currently known by him and his community. That effort indicates that the position of the four documents was not yet inviolably secure. Other portions of what is now our New Testament which circulated as separate collections before they were all combined were the Pastoral Epistles (1 and 2 Timothy, Titus) and the Catholic Epistles (James, 1 and 2 Peter, 1, 2 and 3 John, Jude).

Throughout the third and into the fourth centuries C.E. the process of sifting and the search for consensus extended. Churches in some areas preferred certain Christian writings while others were favored elsewhere.

Eusebius, a fourth century church historian who wrote his *Ecclesiastical History* in 325 C.E., divided the Christian literature currently in use in the churches into four categories: acknowledged, disputed but to be accepted, disputed but to be rejected, heretical. We need not go into more detail except to note that all four Gospels in our New Testament were included in his "acknowledged" category. His "disputed but to be rejected" category included the Acts of Paul, the Shepherd of Hermas, the Didache, the Gospel According to the Hebrews. That indicates that all of the works in that category were being regarded and used as authoritative Scriptures by some Christians in his day. He also included the book of Revelation in that disputed category. This indicates that Christians were ambivalent about its value well into the fourth century.

Toward the end of that century we find evidence that a consensus had begun to emerge. Athanasius, a famous churchman from Alexandria, wrote a festal letter at Easter in 367 C.E. He included a list of Christian writings which he considered authoritative. That list corresponds to the documents which are in our New Testament today. A church council at Hippo (in 393 C.E.) and the Synod of Carthage (397 C.E.) both issued lists of the same Christian writings.

By the beginning of the fifth century the issue was settled for most Christians. We should note, however, that no formal decision was made either by a bishop or by a church council to decide the contents of the New Testament officially for the whole church. Christians came to be of one mind gradually. The criteria by which they reached this consensus seemed to include (1) apostolicity (documents written by an "apostle" or someone intimately associated with an apostle),[21] (2) the soundness of the Christian doctrine the documents contained, and (3) their acceptance for informing the churches' worship, faith, and life (the extent to which they had proven useful for more Christians over a longer period of time than had other Christian documents).

When Jerome published his new Latin translation of the Bible, the Vulgate (c. 390 C.E.), he included the same twenty-seven books. He did have reservations about Hebrews, James, and Revelation, but included them because of their antiquity and their long use. It is of passing interest to note that he included in his Bible the longer list of Jewish Scriptures which had been drawn up by the Greek-speaking Jews. That was why his Bible included the "deutero-canonical" books (sometimes also called the Old Testament Apocrypha).

Eventually Jerome's Latin translation supplanted all others as the standard version of the Bible for Western Christianity. Eastern Orthodoxy continued to struggle over the inclusion of some disputed books. The book of Revelation (the Apocalypse of John), for example, was not finally accepted there until well into the tenth century C.E.

Although from time to time scholars discussed the canon of the Bible (for example, Augustine and Thomas Aquinas), it was not a major issue for Western Christianity for one thousand years.

The rise of humanism, a revival of the study of classical authors, toward the end of the fifteenth century stimulated scholars such as Erasmus and Cardinal Cajetan to question the inclusion of Hebrews, James, Jude, and Revelation in the Bible. During the sixteenth century Reformation, Martin Luther translated the Bible into German. He chose as his guide for the Old Testament the shorter list of documents which the ancient rabbis had approved for the use of Aramaic-speaking Jews. He also listed Hebrews, James, Jude, and Revelation as an appendix to the New Testament. He did not think they should be accorded the same authority as the other New Testament books.

To counteract this influence of the Reformers, church officials at the Council of Trent (1546) declared the books of the Bible as they were contained in the Latin Vulgate to be canonical. Only with this decree was the canon of the Bible officially defined. That definition still describes the scope of the Bible for Roman Catholics today. Various Protestant denominations have defined explicitly their version of the official canon of the Bible also.[22] But for many English-speaking Protestants the canon of the Bible consists of an unofficially defined consensus to accept the books which were included in the King James Version of the Bible (translated in 1611) as authoritative.

V. THE AUTHORITY OF THE GOSPELS

When we raise the question of the authority of the Bible the entire process which produced the Bible and which we have been tracing together must be kept in mind.

A. Terminology

Part of our difficulty in talking about the authority of the Bible is the ambiguity of the terms we use. The Bible is the word of God. It is his inspired revelation. What do those statements mean? Perhaps it will be helpful, then, for us to review definitions of some crucial terms.

1) *Scripture*—from the Latin: scriptum. It means "writings," then, as a technical term, "religious writings." We should avoid automatically equating it with the Bible, disregarding the religious persua-

sion of those to whom we are talking. There are Buddhist Scriptures, Mormon Scriptures, Islamic Scriptures as well as Jewish and Christian Scriptures. All of the books in the Bible are Scriptures, but not all Jewish and Christian Scriptures are included in the Bible.

2) *Bible*—from the Greek: biblia, biblos. It means "written pages, book," then, as a technical term, *"the* book containing (our) Scriptures." We should be aware that the contents of the Bible differ depending on whether a person is a Protestant, or a Roman Catholic, or a Reformed Jew.

3) *Revelation*—means "disclosure, divulgence." It is the act of making known what is obscure or hidden. In the Judaeo-Christian tradition this act properly belongs to God. God is the author of revelation; he is also the content of revelation. Revelation is his divine self-disclosure. The Bible is God's revelation only in a derivative sense. Insofar as it serves as the means through which God makes himself known it is God's revelation. God does not limit his revelation to the Bible.

4) *Word of God*—is God's self-communication. It is the means by which God accomplishes his purposes. As God created through his word so God recreates through his word. That is why Christians know Jesus as "the Word of God." The Bible is the Word of God only in a derivative sense. It is the record of human testimony to the experience of God's self-communication.

5) *Authority*—is the demonstrable trustworthiness of a thing or person. It is capable of convincing a person of truth, or of causing a person to accept a command as valid and binding. Theologically, all authority belongs ultimately to God. He is the one who conveys (who *is*) truth; he compels obedience. The Christian Bible has authority only to the extent that it is the revealed word of God (see the definitions above).

6) *Inspiration*—means literally "the breathing into." Its figurative use with regard to the Christian Scriptures refers to the divine impulse with which God stimulates persons to accomplish tasks. Some Chris-

tians understand inspiration in the limited, technical sense of that divine impulse which resulted in the composition of the documents in the Bible. Other Christians use it in a more general sense to include not just the divine guidance of the writing of books in the Bible but also the writing of other early Christian Scriptures, the decisions of church councils, the definition of the canon, the composition of hymns, the preaching of sermons, and acts of Christian compassion, etc., up to and including contemporary experience.

7) *Literal*—means there are no figurative expressions. Few people who claim that they believe the Bible literally really mean that. Technically, literal belief in the Bible would exclude the use of symbolism or metaphor. When people say that they usually mean that the Bible is inerrant.

8) *Inerrant*—means that there is no error whatsoever in anything that the Bible says. The Bible is not a book on history or astronomy or physics. But when it makes a historical or astronomical or physical observation, it is accurate.

9) *Infallible*—This term can, and for some people does, mean the exact same thing as inerrancy. Others who are uncomfortable with the rigidity of the concept of inerrancy use the term "infallible" to express their conviction that the Bible does not mislead people in matters pertaining to the Christian faith.

From the above definitions we can see that it is very important for us to be precise in identifying our intent when we use these terms to talk about the nature of the Bible. Furthermore, the "truth" of the Bible is finally accessible only to those who share the same faith presuppositions.

What does it mean for Christians to acknowledge the authority of the Bible? There is no single answer since different Christians would answer the question in different ways. Yet there is some commonality since all Christians regard approximately the same collection of early Christian writings as peculiarly normative for Christian doctrine, worship, and practice. In that sense present-day Christians join in and give their assent to that process which we have described above as the formation of the canon.

B. Proven Usefulness

We saw that the early Christians remembered and passed on stories about Jesus, told by the eyewitness disciples and others of the first Christians, which proved useful for worship, preaching, teaching, and counsel. They selected certain stories from the total number of stories that were available. We encountered that same kind of selectivity as we observed the modifications (and the omissions) which Matthew and Luke made on Mark's material. The church simply extended that principle of selectivity according to proven usefulness when it allowed consideration of the acceptance by the churches to influence its choice of which documents belonged in the New Testament. Christians today who acknowledge the authority of the canon of the New Testament as it has been defined affirm the validity of that test.

Contemporary Christians employ the process of selectivity more actively, however, than simply through their recognition and affirmation of that ancient activity. As circumstances change some portions of the biblical writings carry more compelling force than do others.

During times of crisis (for example, the war years of World War II) Christians on both "sides" found the encouragement and assurances of the book of Revelation particularly meaningful. As our nation grappled with issues of social and political morality the ancient words of the Jewish prophets rang out with vivid freshness:

> Let justice roll down like waters,
>   and righteousness like an everflowing stream.
>   (Amos 5:24)

Efforts to reverse the erosion of ethical integrity in the cultures of the twentieth century cause Christians today to return again and again to the biblical passages of ethical admonition.

We employ an "ad hoc" sort of selectivity according to the needs or problems of the Christian community. Those needs drive us to dwell repeatedly on some portions of the Bible to the neglect or, maybe even, the temporary exclusion of other portions. We apply a kind of "canon within the canon" according to how we perceive the biblical texts to converge with our contemporary situations.

C. Sound Doctrine

Early Christians selected and retold Jesus stories to illustrate and clarify their preaching. It follows that they preferred those stories which reflected most nearly their own understanding of who Jesus was and what he was about. Luke modified Mark's narrative of Jesus, changing some of its emphases, omitting some of its material, adding a considerable amount of additional material, so that his revised and extended narrative reflected his theology. The later church was doing the same thing when it tested the suitability of early Christian documents for inclusion into the canon according to their soundness of doctrine. Today Christians give their consent to that evaluation of sound teaching which guided early Christians to discriminate between the New Testament documents and other Christian literature.

Christians today exercise selectivity according to doctrinal content following the example of the ancient Christians. They tend to concentrate upon and emphasize those portions of the Bible which reflect and support their theological interests. Again we can refer to the application of a "canon within the canon" which is determined by confessional or denominational interests. Christians whose theological heritage has been influenced strongly by the writings of the Apostle Paul identify "justification by faith alone" as the "canon within the canon." Other Christians place special stress on the Pastoral Epistles because those documents are fundamental to their type of church government and order. When the sacraments are viewed as central to Christian worship those Christians give special weight to the biblical narratives which nurture their sacramental appreciation. Charismatic Christians turn again and again to the Pentecost narrative of Acts 2 and Paul's discussion of gifts of the Spirit (Charismata) in 1 Corinthians 12—14.

In the words of one scholar "no Christian church or group has in the event treated the NT writings as uniformly canonical. Whatever the theory of canonicity, the reality is that *all Christians have operated with a canon within the canon.* "[23] It is very important that we be neither outraged nor disdainful because of this recognition. When the church defined the canon it included side-by-side documents with diverse perspectives. As in the case of our Gospels it even included, as complementary, documents which originally were designed to replace each other. When the church defined the canon it affirmed the validity of pluralism, and thereby both celebrated and encouraged Christian diversity. The limits of the canon correspond to the church's setting of the borders for legitimate diversity.

D. Apostolicity

The issue of apostolicity is more difficult. Christians for eighteen hundred years believed that the first Gospel was written by the Apostle Matthew Levi and the Fourth Gospel by the Apostle John, the son of Zebedee. Mark was thought to have been the Apostle Peter's assistant while Luke was the missionary companion of the Apostle Paul. Today scholars recognize that all four Gospels are anonymous works. They further find substantive internal reasons for doubting the accuracy of the traditional view of the authors' identities.

We may suspect that apostolicity was not absolutely critical for early Christians. With their high regard for the Gospels of Mark and Luke Christians were quick to make qualifications as to the requirement for apostolic authorship. That the Apostle Paul composed the letter to the Hebrews was quite early and openly doubted. Yet it was still included in the New Testament. Furthermore they excluded many supposedly "apostolic" writings.

We can demonstrate the tentativeness and inadequacy of the claim to apostolicity with an imaginary example. Suppose a third letter from Paul to Corinth was discovered, or a copy of a hitherto unknown Gospel According to Judas, the son of James (cf. Acts 1:13). Suppose there was absolutely no question about their authorship. They proved to be authentic according to all of the tests which scholars now know to apply. Would either new-found document be included into the New Testament of the Bible?

Roman Catholics would be inclined to exclude them. At least the decision made at the Council of Trent (1546) which defined the canon as "closed" (=no more books could be added) would have to be reconsidered. But it would not be an automatic matter for Protestants, who still consider the canon "open" (on the theory that God's Spirit may always say something new). They would want to test the thought, that is, the doctrine of the document first. Undoubtedly there would be an extended interval when the issue of inclusion was in dispute. Finally, after Christians had had opportunity to become acquainted with the document, compare its teachings with the present New Testament documents, and experience its contribution to the quality of their faith and experience, inclusion could be considered. Presumably a council would be called and a vote taken. (One would only hope that yet another new denomination would not be formed though the history of Protestantism gives small assurance.)

The implicit consensus of the church concerning what books to include in the New Testament, which later received official sanction, raised another problem. The church identified and set aside certain documents as authoritative and normative for the life of the church. We have seen that this decision occurred for our Gospels quite early. That decision shifted the focus of the church's doctrine and preaching. The basis for later proclamation and instruction was no longer the event of Jesus' crucifixion and resurrection. The stories about Jesus had been remembered at first to illuminate the preaching of that event. With the formation of the canon the stories themselves became the basis for proclamation. By setting the four Gospels into a specially authoritative category the church chose and made normative four specific stages in the process of adapting the Jesus stories to clarify the Jesus event.

When the church made this decision it set for itself at least two crucial tasks. First, it must continually test and demonstrate the enduring validity of the Gospel stories to reflect faithfully the event the evangelists intended for them to illumine. The new quest for the historical Jesus is concerned with this task.[24]

The second task with which the decision of the canon confronts the church is the interpretive task. The church needs to understand those stories in their historical settings and to faithfully recast their testimony to the event of Jesus into contemporary forms and categories of meaning. Clergy who preach, theologians who teach, Christians who study and reflect on the Gospels' stories as they influence their faith and life all are engaged in this task.

Notes

CHAPTER ONE

1. For a concise assessment of how little is known of this period see Samuel Sandmel, *The First Christian Century in Judaism and Christianity: Certainties and Uncertainties* (New York: Oxford University Press, 1969).
2. The richest and most dependable sources for information about the primitive church are the epistles of Paul. Acts also is tremendously helpful though its information must be examined with more caution.
3. See Etienne Trocmé, *Jesus and His Contemporaries* (London: SCM Press, Ltd., 1973).
4. The earliest listing of these appearances is found in 1 Corinthians 15:5–8. The last of verses 6 and 8 was composed by Paul himself but the remainder is a very early Christian tradition which predates Paul.
5. William Barclay, *Introduction to the First Three Gospels* (Philadelphia: The Westminster Press, 1975), p. 29.
6. Reginald H. Fuller, *The Foundations of New Testament Christology* (New York: Charles Scribner's Sons, 1965) successfully employed the differences in these stages of early Christianity to illumine his examination of the differing emphases in the development of the doctrines of Christ in the New Testament church.
7. Calvin J. Roetzel, *The Letters of Paul: Conversations in Context* (Atlanta: John Knox Press, 1975).
8. Willi Marxsen, *Introduction to the New Testament*, trans. G. Buswell (Oxford: Basil Blackwell, 1968), p. 126.
9. Günther Bornkamm, *The New Testament: A Guide to Its Writings* (Philadelphia: Fortress Press, 1973), p. 40.
10. The best known early form-critical studies of the Gospel traditions were: Martin Dibelius, *From Tradition to Gospel* (Greenwood, South Carolina: The Attic Press, Inc., 1971); Rudolf Bultmann, *The History of the Synoptic Tradition* (Oxford: Basil Blackwell, 1963); Vincent Taylor, *The Formation of the Gospel Tradition* (London: Macmillan and Co., Limited, 1953). Dibelius was first published in 1919, Bultmann in 1921 and Taylor in 1933.
11. W. D. Davies, *Invitation to the New Testament: A Guide to Its Main Witness* (Garden City, N.Y.: Doubleday & Company, Inc., 1966), p. 116.

12. The categories which follow conform essentially to those proposed by Bultmann, *History*, though the nomenclature may vary.
13. Other examples of this kind of expansion may be observed in Mark 3:31–35 where verse 35 interprets verse 34, and Mark 7:20–23 which interprets Mark 7:18–19 which is itself an expansion of Mark 7:15.
14. A convenient list is available in Reginald H. Fuller, *A Critical Introduction to the New Testament* (London: Gerald Duckworth & Co. Ltd., 1966), pp. 85–87.
15. The extremes which this inclination eventually achieved are vividly illustrated in some of the early Christian literature collected by Edgar Hennecke and Wilhelm Schneemelcher, *New Testament Apocrypha*, trans. A. J. B. Higgins, 2 vols. (Philadelphia: Westminster Press, 1963).
16. This overview is dependent on the analysis presented by Bultmann, *History*, pp. 14–16.
17. Unfamiliarity with the type of house construction typical of first century Palestine would prevent Mark from recognizing that such buildings ordinarily had a roof opening which could be used for entry.
18. An extended discussion of this category together with numerous illustrations from the New Testament may be found in Barclay, *Introduction*, pp. 42ff.
19. Form criticism stimulated great and fruitful interest in the study of the parables. Several recent books which have thoroughly investigated this category of the Jesus sayings traditions are C. H. Dodd, *The Parables of the Kingdom* (London: Nisbet & Co., Ltd., 1953); Joachim Jeremias, *The Parables of Jesus*, rev. ed., trans. S. H. Hooke (New York: Charles Scribner, 1963); Eta Linnemann, *Parables of Jesus* (London: S.P.C.K., 1966); Dan Otto Via, *The Parables* (Philadelphia: Fortress Press, 1967); Sallie McFague TeSelle, *Speaking in Parables: A Study in Metaphor and Theology* (Philadelphia: Fortress Press, 1975); Charles E. Carlston, *The Parables of the Triple Tradition* (Philadelphia: Fortress Press, 1975).
20. Barclay, *Introduction*, p. 49.
21. It will be argued that this is the literary relationship between the first three Gospels, pp. 79 ff.
22. Cited by Barclay, *Introduction*, p. 53.
23. Ernst Käsemann has brilliantly defined and investigated a distinct class of sayings which are community formulations in "Sentences of Holy Law in the New Testament," one of the essays included in *New Testament Questions of Today* (London: SCM, 1969).
24. Willi Marxsen, *Mark, the Evangelist: Studies on the Redaction History of*

the Gospel (Nashville: Abingdon Press, 1969), pp. 126 ff., thoroughly investigates Mark's use of the term "gospel."

25. Bornkamm, *Religion in Geschichte und Gegenwart,* 3rd ed. (Tübingen: J. C. B. Mohr, 1958), Vol. II, Col. 749; quoted by Wilhelm Schneemelcher, *New Testament Apocrypha,* trans. A. J. B. Higgins, et al., Vol. I, p. 74.
26. Francis Wright Beare, *The Earliest Records of Jesus* (Oxford: Basil Blackwell, 1962), p. 16.
27. On the Fourth Gospel see Robert Kysar, *John, the Maverick Gospel* (Atlanta: John Knox Press, 1976).

CHAPTER TWO

1. See pp. 80 ff.
2. Insufficient attention to this feature of Markan style led Samuel George Frederick Brandon in *Jesus and the Zealots* (Manchester: Manchester University Press, 1967), p. 333, n. 3, to regard 11:11 as a preliminary reconnoitering foray.
3. Burnett Hillman Streeter, *The Four Gospels: A Study of Origins* (London: Macmillan, 1924), pp. 168, 293, responded to several versions of the "Ur-Marcus" theory and indicated their flaws.
4. Martin Kähler, *The So-Called Historical Jesus and the Historic Biblical Christ,* trans. Carl E. Braaten (Philadelphia: Fortress Press, 1964), p. 80. This is a translation of the second edition of a work which was first published in German in 1892.
5. Etienne Trocmé, *The Formation of the Gospel According to Mark* (Philadelphia: Westminster Press, 1975), pp. 88–119.
6. Theodore J. Weeden, *Mark—Traditions in Conflict* (Philadelphia: Fortress Press, 1971), p. 51. See his perceptive overview of Mark's presentation of the disciples, pp. 23–51.
7. Willi Marxsen, *Introduction,* p. 144.
8. Ibid., pp. 130ff.
9. See James Kallas, *Jesus and the Power of Satan* (Philadelphia: Westminster Press, 1968) for a fuller description of this dimension of Mark's portrayal of Jesus.
10. James L. Price, *Interpreting the New Testament,* 2nd edition (New York: Holt, Rinehart and Winston, Inc., 1971), p. 199.
11. Karl Ludwig Schmidt, *Der Rahmen der Geschichte Jesu* (Berlin: Trowitzsch & Sohn, 1919) argued persuasively for a theological interpretation of Markan geographical designations.
12. Weeden, *Traditions,* has correctly assessed the central function of Peter's

confession and described its christological concerns, pp. 54ff.

13. William Wrede, *The Messianic Secret*, trans. J. C. G. Greig (London: James Clarke and Co., Ltd., 1971—a translation of the 3rd edition of the German original published in 1901), anticipated the concerns of redaction criticism when he attributed the messianic secret motif to Mark's redactional imposition and saw in it a significant clue to Markan theology.

14. See pp. 54.

15. Recently J. A. T. Robinson, *Redating the New Testament* (Philadelphia: The Westminster Press, 1976) has suggested a radical revision for the chronology of New Testament literature by dating all New Testament documents prior to 70 A.D. The success of this suggestion has yet to be assessed.

16. See pp. 69 ff. above.

17. Only Mark 4:26–29; 7:31–37; 8:22–26 and a few scattered individual verses are not found in either Matthew's Gospel or Luke's.

18. A number of different Gospel harmonies are available. One of the most popular is *Gospel Parallels: A Synopsis of the First Three Gospels*, edited by Burton Hamilton Throckmorton, Jr. (Camden, N.J.: Thomas Nelson and Sons, 3rd edition, 1967). See also *Synopsis of the Four Gospels*, ed. Kurt Aland (New York: American Bible Society, 1975), which has the Greek text in parallel columns on one page and the English text of the Revised Standard Version on the facing page.

19. The percentages are calculated from the count of Werner Georg Kümmel, *Introduction to the New Testament*, trans. Howard Clark Kee, 17th ed. (Nashville: Abingdon Press, 1973), p. 57.

20. Of course vocabulary similarity really has to be computed on the basis of the Greek texts of the Synoptic Gospels but most modern English versions reflect vocabulary correspondence and divergence fairly faithfully. The statistics given in the text should be further qualified with the recollection that there is no way to be certain that the wording preserved in extant Greek manuscripts (the earliest of them date from the third century) preserves the precise wording of the originals. During the process of textual transmission it is probable that errors in copying or intentional changes were made (which would reduce the rate of vocabulary agreement from that of the original documents), and that some accommodation would occur to bring originally disparate texts into conformity (which would increase the rate of vocabulary agreement). It should also be remembered that in an oral culture, traditions which are regarded as especially significant—especially important sayings—become stereo-

typed and fixed while still being transmitted orally, which would tend to inflate the rate of correspondence in the "words of Jesus" material.

21. William Reuben Farmer, *The Synoptic Problem* (New York: The Macmillan Co., 1964); see also Basil Christopher Butler, *The Originality of St. Matthew: A Critique of the Two-Document Hypothesis* (Cambridge: The University Press, 1951). No one seems to be inclined to tackle the monumental problems involved in proposing the priority of Luke.

22. G. M. Styler, "The Priority of Mark" in C. F. D. Moule, *The Birth of the New Testament* (London: Adam and Charles Black, 2nd ed., 1966), pp. 223–232.

23. Other passages Styler discussed that contain Matthean misunderstandings which presume knowledge of the Markan narrative are Matthew 9:4, compare Mark 2:18—a confusion about who Mark's "they" are; Matthew 13:10–15, compare Mark 4:10–12—a Matthean attempt to make sense out of the intolerable but inaccurate reading of Mark to the effect that Jesus taught in parables to confuse; Matthew 16:5–12, compare Mark 8:14–21—Matthew misinterpreted "leaven" to be a reference to the teaching of the religious leaders (Matt. 16:12).

24. See p. 78 ff.

25. Streeter, *The Four Gospels,* pp. 208ff.

26. An alternate tradition attributes the symbol to Armitage Robinson, cf. Barclay, *Introduction,* p. 95; Richard A. Edwards, *A Theology of Q: Eschatology, Prophecy, and Wisdom* (Philadelphia: Fortress Press, 1976), p. 2, n. 2.

27. Lest this observation should be overvalued, however, one has only to recall the wide variance in the Lord's Prayer tradition (Luke 11:1–4 and parallel) and the Last Supper tradition (Luke 22:15–20 and parallel), both of which were presumably central to the cultic worship of the early church, to be warned against simplistic insistance on the dependability of memorized oral traditions.

28. To my knowledge this possibility has not been given the consideration it deserves with reference to the Lukan passion narrative.

29. See the description of this category of oral traditions forms in the first chapter, pp. 41 ff.

30. Edwards, *Theology,* chapters 3–5.

31. The list is taken from ibid., pp. xi-xiii, though the columns of citations have been transposed. The citations from Mark's Gospel are included to indicate those traditions for which the correspondence of detail between Matthew and Luke diverges so sharply from Mark that the presence of the same general tradition in both written sources, Mark and Q, seems

likely. Copyright © 1976 by Fortress Press. Reprinted by permission of Fortress Press.

32. Ibid., p. 10. He is referring to Taylor's essay "The Original Order of Q," *New Testament Essays: Studies in Memory of Thomas Walter Manson, 1893–1958,* ed. Angus John Brockhurst Higgins (Manchester: University of Manchester Press, 1959).

33. Edwards, pp. 146, 148–149.

34. Cf. James M. Robinson & Helmut Koester, *Trajectories Through Early Christianity* (Philadelphia: Fortress Press, 1971).

CHAPTER THREE

1. See pp. 80 ff.

2. See pp. 83 ff.

3. Pp. 86 f.

4. Discussed on pp. 50 f.

5. See p. 102 f.

6. Luke apparently knew of a different tradition about the death of Judas, cf. Acts 1:18–19.

7. A complete list of Matthew's special material is given by Sherman E. Johnson in the "Introduction" of "The Gospel According to St. Matthew," *The Interpreter's Bible* (Nashville: Abingdon-Cokesbury, 1951), Vol. 7, p. 238.

8. This aspect of Matthew's use of Old Testament quotations is thoroughly explored by W. F. Albright & C. S. Mann, *Matthew* (Garden City, New York: Doubleday & Co., 1971), pp. LXIIff., who took too seriously a suggestion made by C. H. Dodd, *According to the Scriptures* (New York: Scribner, 1953).

9. Matthew probably erred in ascribing the tradition to Jeremiah. His version is not a direct quotation in any event.

10. Although Marxsen, *Introduction,* p. 147, considers Matthew's use of the prophecy-fulfillment pattern original, it is discernible even in the writings of Paul. Norman Perrin, *The New Testament: An Introduction* (New York: Harcourt Brace Jovanovich, Inc., 1974), p. 173, is probably accurate in regarding its use in Matthew as intensification of "a commonplace of Christian apologetic."

11. While the distinctive presence of the five discourses is too obvious to be ignored the view stimulated by Benjamin Wisner Bacon, *Studies in Matthew* (London: Constable, 1930), and frequently urged since, that Matthew intended to effect a correspondence and even to replace the five

books of the Torah (the Pentateuch) with the five discourses of Jesus is too extreme.

12. Cf. Davies, *Invitation,* p. 214.

13. The chart is adapted from the one given by David L. Barr in "The Drama of Matthew's Gospel: A Reconsideration of Its Structure and Purpose," *Theology Digest,* 24:4 (Winter 1976), pp. 354–355. Reprinted by permission.

14. Both the Gospel of John and the book of Revelation depend heavily on the method of concentrically developed themes, also.

15. Peter F. Ellis, *Matthew: His Mind and His Message* (Collegeville, Minnesota: The Liturgical Press, 1974), pp. 20–22, traces seven themes in the Great Commission alone and their frequent recurrence in the five major discourses.

16. Barclay, *Introduction,* p. 161.

17. Discussed above, pp. 102 f.

18. That the last group contains, strictly speaking, only thirteen names in the generations list confirms that the pattern described in verse 17 was imposed on the genealogy tradition. This list has been abridged from the one given by W. F. Albright & C. S. Mann, *The Anchor Bible: Matthew: Introduction, Translation, and Notes* (Garden City, N.Y.: Doubleday and Co., 1971), pp. LVII-LVIII.

19. "The formal arrangement of Matthew's gospel is an alternating sequence of narrative and discourse sections in the pattern: N-D-N-D-N-D-N-D-N-D-N." D. B. Barr, "The Drama," p. 351.

20. See the chart on p. 104 above.

21. J. D. Kingsbury, *The Parables of Jesus in Matthew 13* (Richmond, Va.: John Knox Press, 1969), persuasively argued for the central significance of this chapter for the Gospel of Matthew.

22. The description of the pattern is adapted from the one by Peter F. Ellis, *Matthew,* p. 12.

23. Kingsbury, *Parables,* pp. 12–15 describes a parallel relationship between the two halves of the chapter, which he defines later as respectively apologetic and paranaetic.

24. See especially Jack Dean Kingsbury, *Matthew: Structure, Christology, Kingdom* (Philadelphia: Fortress Press, 1975); cf. also Kümmel, *Introduction,* p. 105.

25. Perrin, *Introduction,* p. 173.

26. This experience was not encountered everywhere. Paul testified that during his missionary activity (in the 40s and 50s C.E.) he had encountered strident hostility from Jews (2 Cor. 11:24–26; Rom. 15:31) and had,

himself, been an agent of persecution against the church at one time (Gal. 1:13).

27. Note particularly Matthew's explicit interpretation of the parable of the wicked tenants in verse 43. Neither Mark nor Luke has this verse.

28. O. Lamar Cope, *Matthew: A Scribe Trained for the Kingdom of Heaven* (Washington, D.C.: Catholic Biblical Association of America, 1976), p. 128.

29. As quoted by G. D. Kilpatrick, *The Origins of the Gospel According to St. Matthew* (Oxford: Clarendon Press, 1946), p. 109.

CHAPTER FOUR

1. These figures exclude the epistle to the Hebrews which is not ordinarily included in the Pauline corpus any longer.

2. Although the usual title for this companion work is used, it is unfortunately phrased. The title should reflect the centrality which the activity of the Holy Spirit has in the Acts narrative, or better, the continuing exercise by the exalted Jesus of his authority in his church by means of the Holy Spirit.

3. Nils Alstrup Dahl, "The Purpose of Luke-Acts," *Jesus in the Memory of the Early Church* (Minneapolis: Augsburg, 1976), p. 88.

4. See Marxsen's discussion, *Introduction*, pp. 156–157.

5. Kümmel, *Introduction*, p. 142.

6. For a more detailed list see Charles H. Talbert, *Literary Patterns, Theological Themes, and the Genre of Luke-Acts* (Missoula, Montana: Scholars Press, 1975), pp. 15–23.

7. Cf. Talbert, ibid., pp. 98–99.

8. See p. 95.

9. For a description of the two positions as well as some of the literature contributing to the debate see Hans Conzelmann, *The Theology of St. Luke* New York: Harper and Row, 1960), pp. 52–55.

10. See pp. 96 for an explanation of "historical present."

11. "Imperfect" and "aorist" are both past tense forms of the Greek verb. When an action which had been completed in the past was intended, the use of the aorist was literarily correct.

12. For further discussion on this point consult Kümmel, *Introduction*, pp. 148–149.

13. See pp. 130 f.

14. The list is based on the one given by Barclay, *Introduction*, p. 215. For

a more complete listing of Luke's special materials see Price, *Interpreting*, pp. 217–218.

15. The ahistorical character of Mark's Gospel was convincingly described by Karl Ludwig Schmidt, *Rahmen der Geschichte Jesu* (Berlin: Trowitzsch & Sohn, 1919).

16. Robert A. Spivey and D. Moody Smith, Jr., *Anatomy of the New Testament* (New York: Macmillan, 1969), p. 142–143.

17. Dahl, "Purpose," p. 93.

18. Ibid., p. 89. Cf. also Luke 9:45; 18:34; 24:25.

19. Some examples of the way Luke toned down references to the nearness of the end of time can be seen by comparing the following texts with their parallels in Mark: Luke 4:14–21; 9:27; 19:11; 21:8–9; 22:69. Nevertheless Luke did not suppress all references to the nearness of the end; cf. Luke 10:9–11; 12:45–46; 18:7–8.

20. On this understanding of history as salvation history and its impact on early Christianity as reflected in the biblical documents, cf. Oscar Cullmann, *Salvation in History* (New York: Harper & Row, 1967).

21. Conzelmann, *The Theology of St. Luke*. Although Luke did not describe the first epoch (it was ably recorded in the Jewish Scriptures), his vivid description of the second and third epochs presumes the first.

22. Perrin, *Introduction*, p. 203.

23. So Irenaeus (c. 185 C.E.) as quoted by Eusebius, *The History of the Church from Christ to Constantine*, trans. G.A. Williamson (New York: Penguin Books, 1965), V:8:3, p. 210; see also the Muratorian Canon (end of 2nd century, C.E.?) in Hennecke and Schneemelcher, *New Testament Apocrypha*, Vol. I, pp. 42–45. Apparently Marcion, another early compiler of Christian literature (c. 150 C.E.) used a modified version of the Third Gospel, cf. Hennecke and Schneemelcher, pp. 32–33.

CHAPTER FIVE

1. Voices have been raised from time to time to warn us of the distorting effect of combining New Testament variety into one view. An earlier work which has attracted renewed interest is Walter Bauer's *Orthodoxy and Heresy in Earliest Christianity* (Philadelphia: Fortress, 1971; the German original was published in 1934). A recent, thorough, and provocative study is James D. G. Dunn, *Unity and Diversity in the New Testament* (Philadelphia: Westminster, 1977).

2. Dunn has done that study admirably—see his work cited in the previous footnote.

3. Albert Schweitzer, *The Quest of the Historical Jesus* (New York: Macmillan, 1964; published in German in 1906), surveyed several major nineteenth century lives of Jesus and ruthlessly exposed their methodological bias.

4. Actually, since we do not have access to the original manuscript of Mark's Gospel the statement in the text is an oversimplification. Scholars, however, who have studied the history of the transmission of ancient texts and who are expert at comparing variant readings to reconstruct the more primitive (original) text encourage us that the uncertainties that remain about the original reading of Mark's narrative are rare and insignificant.

5. Norman Perrin, *Rediscovering the Teaching of Jesus* (New York: Harper and Row, 1967) may profitably be consulted for a lucid expanded discussion of these three criteria. I have depended on him for many points in what follows.

6. Paul knew of this form of address for God, also. See Rom. 8:15; Gal. 4:6.

7. See pp. 161 f.

8. This occurs as an addition after Luke 6:4 in Codex Bezae. The translation is from Bruce M. Metzger, *A Textual Commentary on the Greek New Testament* (New York and London: United Bible Societies, 1971), p. 140.

9. Perrin, *Introduction,* p. 285.

10. Joachim Jeremias, *The Unknown Sayings of Jesus,* trans.. Reginald H. Fuller (London: S.P.C.K., 1958) accumulated all of the "sayings of Jesus" recorded in early Christian literature other than the four Gospels. Primarily on the basis of the criterion of coherence he described twenty-one sayings as having just as much of a claim to authenticity as any of the sayings of Jesus contained in the canonical Gospels.

11. A more extensive and detailed listing may be found in Fuller, *Critical Introduction,* pp. 99–102.

12. *The Apostolic Fathers,* ed. Robert McQueen Grant (New York: Thomas Nelson and Sons, 1964–1968, 6 vols.) provides a very readable translation of this literature together with a helpful commentary.

13. The manuscript is called Codex Sinaiticus, so named because it was discovered in the middle of the nineteenth century in a monastary at the base of what has traditionally been identified as Mount Sinai.

14. The best collection of this literature is the two volume *The New Testament Apocrypha* edited by Hennecke and Schneemelcher.

15. Ibid., Vol. II, pp. 383–387.

16. Hennecke and Schneemelcher lists over forty.

17. The translation of Thomas is from *Synopsis quattuor Evangeliorum,* ed. Kurt Aland (Stuttgart: Würtembergische Bibelanstalt, 1964), p. 529.

18. G Pet 9–10; Hennecke and Schneelmelcher, Vol. I, pp. 185–186.
19. A recently published translation of the entire collection together with an introduction briefly describing the history and scope of the find is *The Nag Hammadi Library* edited by James M. Robinson (New York: Harper and Row, 1977).
20. Papias wrote this in the preface to a lost five-volume collection of Jesus sayings. Eusebius quoted from the preface in his *The History of the Church from Christ to Constantine* 3:39:2–3, p. 150.
21. We should note that scholars today agree only on the apostolic authorship of the letters of Paul. And he, of course, was not one of the eyewitness disciples who accompanied Jesus during his earthly ministry.
22. One such example is the list contained in the Westminster Confession of Faith, I:2, originally adopted in 1648, and still definitive for most Presbyterians.
23. Dunn, *Unity and Diversity,* p. 374.
24. See pp. 157 ff.

Bibliography

Aland, Kurt, ed. *Synopsis of the Four Gospels.* New York: American Bible Society, 1975.

———. *Synopsis quattuor Evangeliorum.* Stuttgart: Würtembergische Bibelanstalt, 1964.

Albright, William F., and Mann, C. S., eds. *Anchor Bible: Matthew.* Garden City, N.Y.: Doubleday and Co., 1971.

Bacon, Benjamin W. *Studies in Matthew.* London: Constable, 1930.

Barclay, William. *Introduction to the First Three Gospels.* Philadelphia: The Westminster Press, 1975.

Barr, David L. "The Drama of Matthew's Gospel: A Reconsideration of Its Structure and Purpose," *Theology Digest.* 24:4, 1976.

Bauer, Walter. *Orthodoxy and Heresy in Earliest Christianity.* Philadelphia: Fortress, 1971.

Beare, Frank W. *The Earliest Records of Jesus.* Oxford: Basil Blackwell, 1962.

Bornkamm, Günther. *The New Testament: A Guide to Its Writings.* Philadelphia: Fortress Press, 1973.

Brandon, S. G. F. *Jesus and the Zealots.* Manchester: Manchester University Press, 1967.

Bultmann, Rudolf. *The History of the Synoptic Tradition.* Oxford: Basil Blackwell, 1963.

Butler, B. C. *The Originality of St. Matthew.* Cambridge: The University Press, 1951.

Carlston, Charles E. *The Parables of the Triple Tradition.* Philadelphia: Fortress Press, 1975.

Conzelmann, Hans. *The Theology of St. Luke.* New York: Harper and Row, 1960.

Cope, O. Lamar. *Matthew: A Scribe Trained for the Kingdom of Heaven.* Washington, D.C.: Catholic Biblical Association of America, 1976.

Cullmann, Oscar. *Salvation in History.* New York: Harper & Row, 1967.

Dahl, Nils A. "The Purpose of Luke Acts," *Jesus in the Memory of the Early Church.* Minneapolis: Augsburg, 1976.

Davis, William David. *Invitation to the New Testament.* Garden City, N.Y.: Doubleday, 1969.

Dibelius, Martin. *From Tradition to Gospel.* Greenwood, South Carolina: The Attic Press, Inc., 1971.

Dodd, C. H. *According to the Scriptures.* New York: Scribner, 1953.

———. *The Parables of the Kingdom.* London: Nisbet & Co., Ltd., 1953.

Dunn, James D. G. *Unity and Diversity in the New Testament.* Philadelphia: Westminister, 1977.

Edwards, Richard Alan. *A Theology of Q: Eschatology, Prophecy, and Wisdom.* Philadelphia: Fortress Press, 1976.

Ellis, Peter F. *Matthew: His Mind and His Message.* Collegeville, Minnesota: The Liturgical Press, 1974.

Farmer, William R. *The Synoptic Problem: A Critical Analysis.* New York: The Macmillan Co., 1964.

Fuller, Reginald H. *A Critical Introduction to the New Testament.* London: Duckworth, 1966.

————. *The Foundations of New Testament Christology.* New York: Charles Scribner's Sons, 1965.

Grant, Robert M., ed. *The Apostolic Fathers: A New Translation and Commentary.* New York: Thomas Nelson and Sons, 1964–1968.

Hennecke, Edgar and Schneemelcher, Wilhelm. *New Testament Apocrypha.* 2 vols. Philadelphia: Westminster Press, 1963.

Higgins, A. J. B., ed. *New Testament Essays: Studies in Memory of Thomas Walter Manson, 1893–1958.* Manchester: Manchester University Press, 1959.

Jeremias, Joachim. *The Parables of Jesus,* rev. ed. New York: Charles Scribner, 1963.

————. *The Unknown Sayings of Jesus.* London: S.P.C.K., 1958.

Johnson, Sherman E. "The Gospel According to St. Matthew," *The Interpreter's Bible.* Nashville: Abingdon-Cokesbury, 1951.

Kähler, Martin. *The So-Called Historical Jesus and the Historic Biblical Christ.* Philadelphia: Fortress Press, 1964.

Kallas, James. *Jesus and the Power of Satan.* Philadelphia: Westminister Press, 1968.

Käsemann, Ernst. *New Testament Questions of Today.* London: SCM, 1969.

Kilpatrick, G. D. *The Origins of the Gospel According to St. Matthew.* Oxford: Clarendon Press, 1946.

Kingsbury, Jack Dean. *Matthew: Structure, Christology, Kingdom.* Philadelphia: Fortress Press, 1975.

————. *The Parables of Jesus in Matthew 13.* Richmond, Virginia: John Knox Press, 1969.

Kümmel, Werner Georg. *Introduction to the New Testament.* 17th ed. Nashville: Abingdon Press, 1973.

Kysar, Robert. *John, the Maverick Gospel.* Atlanta: John Knox Press, 1976.

Linnemann, Eta. *Parables of Jesus: Introduction and Exposition.* London: S.P.C.K., 1966.

Marxsen, Willi. *Introduction to the New Testament: An Approach to Its Problems.* Oxford: Basil Blackwell, 1968.

————. *Mark, the Evangelist.* Nashville: Abingdon Press, 1966.

Metzger, Bruce M. *A Textual Commentary on the Greek New Testament.*

New York and London: United Bible Societies, 1971.

Moule, C.F.D. *The Birth of the New Testament.* London: Adam and Charles Black (wnd ed.), 1966.

Perrin, Norman. *Rediscovering the Teaching of Jesus.* New York: Harper and Row, 1967.

————. *The New Testament: An Introduction.* Chicago: Harcourt, Brace, Jovanovich, 1974.

Price, James L. *Interpreting the New Testament.* 2nd ed. New York: Holt, Rinehart and Winston, Inc., 1971.

Robinson, James M. and Koester, Helmut. *Trajectories Through Early Christianity.* Philadelphia: Fortress Press, 1971.

Robinson, J.A.T. *Redating the New Testament.* Philadelphia: The Westminster Press, 1976.

Roetzel, Calvin J. *The Letters of Paul: Conversations in Context.* Atlanta: John Knox Press, 1975.

Sandmel, Samuel. *The First Christian Century in Judaism and Christianity: Certainties and Uncertainties.* New York: Oxford University Press, 1969.

Schmidt, Karl Ludwig. *Der Rahmen der Geschichte Jesu.* Berlin: Trowitzsch & Sohn, 1919.

————. *Rahmen der Geschichte Jesu.* Berlin: Trowitzsch & Sohn, 1919.

Schweitzer, Albert. *The Quest of the Historical Jesus.* New York: Macmillan, 1964.

Spivey, Robert A., and Smith D. Moody, Jr. *Anatomy of the New Testament.* New York: Macmillan, 1969.

Streeter, B. H. *The Four Gospels: A Study of Christian Origins.* New York: Macmillan, 1926.

Talbert, Charles H. *Literary Patterns, Theological Themes, and the Genre of Luke-Acts.* Missoula, Montana: Scholars Press, 1974.

Taylor, Vincent. *The Formation of the Gospel Tradition.* London: Macmillan and Co., Limited, 1953.

TeSelle, Sallie. *Speaking in Parables.* Philadelphia: Fortress Press, 1975.

Throckmorton, B. H., Jr., ed. *Gospel Parallels: A Synopsis of the First Three Gospels.* Camden, N.J.: Thomas Nelson and Sons, 1957.

Trocmé, Etienne. *Jesus and His Contemporaries.* London: SCM Press, Ltd., 1973.

————. *The Formation of the Gospel According to Mark.* Philadelphia: Fortress Press, 1964.

Via, Dan O. *The Parables: Their Literary and Existential Dimension.* Philadelphia: Fortress Press, 1967.

Weeden, Theodore J. *Mark: Traditions in Conflict.* Philadelphia: Fortress Press, 1971.

Wrede, William. *The Messianic Secret.* London: James Clarke and Co., Ltd., 1971.